AS GOOD
AS ANY MAN

To Ian Martin, Archivist, King's Own Scottish Borderers.
Without whose enthusiasm and support this work
would never have been published.

AS GOOD
AS ANY MAN

SCOTLAND'S BLACK TOMMY

MORAG MILLER, ROY LAYCOCK,
JOHN SADLER AND ROSIE SERDIVILLE

Cover image: Arthur Roberts (Morag Miller and Roy Laycock)

First published 2014

The History Press
The Mill, Brimscombe Port
Stroud, Gloucestershire, GL5 2QG
www.thehistorypress.co.uk

British Library Cataloguing in Publication Data.
A catalogue record for this book is available from the British Library.

ISBN 978 0 7509 5374 0

Typesetting and origination by The History Press
Printed in Great Britain

No black no white, No good no bad, There stood glory, There fell fate …

Arthur William David Roberts (1897–1982)

One hundred years have passed,
Still the blame goes on,
No black no white,
No good no bad,
There stood glory,
There fell fate,
Where was sense,
Where was shame,
But never forget,
Those who gave,
Their todays,
For our tomorrows,
Nor those who lived,
And bore the scars for life.

Roy Laycock: *1914* (2012)

CONTENTS

ACKNOWLEDGEMENTS

This book could never have been written without the detailed research and background work undertaken by Morag Thomson Miller and Roy Laycock. It is their dedication and diligence that has steadily built up Arthur's story from the time of its chance discovery. Thanks are also due to Chloe Rodham for the maps, Ian Martin, curator of the King's Own Scottish Borderers Museum in Berwick, Murray Miller, Laura Smith, the owners of Arthur's memorabilia, Doreen Thomas, Darryl Gwynne and family, Lauren Crooks, Ian McCracken, Rita Thomas, Craig Fleming, Tony Sharkey, Steve Wallwork, Marc Rath, James Beal, Sarah Taylor, Janet Hiscocks, the Bristol Archivists, Karen Greenshields, Ruth Alexander, Izzy Charman from Media, Allison O'Neill, Jim and Isa Wilson, personal acquaintances of Arthur, Alan Bullas, for photographs, Glasgow Registry Office, The Mitchell Library, Glasgow, Thos Robertson, Wendy L.T. Miller, Christine Hughes, Jane Rafferty, Sandy Leishman, Bob Steele, Pat Docherty, Frank Leonard, Gus McPherson and Jean Mackenzie, staff at the Glasgow City Archives, Jim Fleming, and, finally, to Mark Beynon and the editorial staff at The History Press for another successful collaboration.

***

I should like it to be clearly understood that in writing this miniature book of sketches, I lay no claim whatever to possess any literary abilities (Arthur Roberts).

Likewise, any errors or omissions are entirely the responsibility of the joint authors.

Rosie Serdiville, John Sadler, Morag Thomson Miller and Roy Laycock
October 2013

INTRODUCTION:
THE FORGOTTEN

In the autumn of 2004, two young people purchased a house in Mount Vernon, a residential suburb of Glasgow. They had no expectation of undiscovered treasure but there, in the uncleared attic, they found it. Behind a Dansette turntable they discovered a cardboard box. And in that box was Arthur. Arthur William David Roberts, who had died over twenty years previously and whose life story, like a time capsule, had lain forgotten ever since. Here, in his diaries, pictures and memorabilia, was the record of his life. At the core of Arthur lay his war experience; the record of a man who had lived through the cauldron of Flanders during the Third Battle of Ypres in 1917:

> For so short an army career, I think I may safely say, my life during that period was as varied, and eventful, as most private soldiers of a similar length of service. A soldier during war time if capable is pushed into many breaches whether fit for the front line or base. I have been fit for both; consequently I have filled many breaches. The last sentence will perhaps lead the reader to think I am possessed of great capabilities, and this belief may be strengthened when I say that I have been

company-runner, batman, guide, dining-hall attendant, bugler, cycle-orderly, dispatch clerk, bomber, motor mechanic, telephone orderly, aircraft-gunner, hut-builder, stretcher-bearer, and one or two other things. Now it has been unintentional, if I have seemingly blown my own horn about my military accomplishments, but I think this book, written as frankly as I could write it will exonerate me from any imputation of self-aggrandisement.

The strange thing about it is, that according to my discharge, my military qualifications are 'Nil'. At that rate, I think nothing short of being a Commander-in-Chief, allows me to have a military qualification.

There is yet another very strange thing, but this also puzzles me. I have volunteered for detachments, sniping jobs etc., but when the orderly sergeant was looking for volunteers for church parade, Pte. Roberts was talking scandal in the latrine, or was attacked with a generous fit, and was carrying water for the cooks.

Should the parade be compulsory, the same Pte. fell in the extreme rear, trusting to luck that the church hut or tent, would not hold the lot.

The story is a remarkable one. Arthur Roberts was born in Bristol in 1897 of mixed-race parents. David Roberts (Jenkins), his father, a ship's steward, hailed from the Caribbean. His mother, Laura Dann, was a West Country lass. By the time of Arthur's birth, the family had dropped the surname Jenkins. At some point in the early twentieth century it appears Arthur and his father moved to Glasgow, where the young boy was educated. Remaining at school well beyond the normal leaving age of 14, it is clear from the quality of his prose that he was a highly intelligent and articulate young man. The photographs show us a bit of a dandy: he looks directly and confidently out at the world, a young man of style, who invites our interest – traits that would be apparent all his life.

The adult Arthur was a marine engineer who worked for some of Glasgow's largest and most important engineering firms: Harland & Wolff and Duncan Stewart (later Davy United). He volunteered in February 1917, first with the King's Own Scottish Borderers, then, in June of that year, with 2nd Battalion Royal Scots Fusiliers.

Arthur's story is not just another set of Great War memoirs, adding to the considerable volume that already exists, but a unique record from the viewpoint of a mixed-race soldier. Relatively few black soldiers served in a front-line role with Scottish regiments in the First World War. The conflict consumed many lives in Scotland and her proud regiments garnered many laurels – won at a very high price. Arthur Roberts does not dwell on his race or cultural identity – he is very much an individual, both participant and wry observer, slightly detached, while clearly not, in any way, excluded.

Accounts by black soldiers are very rare in Scottish literature. And yet Arthur's narrative is very much a Scottish experience, regardless of the writer's origin. It is extremely well written and beautifully illustrated; the writer was an accomplished artist. It is more than just a war memoir, it is a fully rounded account that has been ably illuminated by Morag Thomson Miller and Roy Laycock, who have painstakingly researched the subject's life history. They know Glasgow intimately as natives and a great part of Arthur's story is his life as an adopted Glaswegian:

I first actually entered the trenches on the dawn of 9th June, 1917. I can tell you, after our gruelling march [described in the diary], I was a physical wreck. That night as I plumped down in a dugout, I was so tired that without taking off my equipment, I almost immediately fell into a trance. All the Kaiser's horses and all the Kaiser's men could not have put the wind up me that night. No, I was too far beyond the stage of self-preservation. Sleep and welcome oblivion was wanted. I believe I should not have cared if I had been told I should never wake up again.

Every year, Remembrance Day on 11 November becomes a more self-conscious event – now almost 'Disneyfied' in the contemporary slush of sentimentality. No future generation will have the privilege of hearing, in person, the voices of those who served, as the last known survivors have died. This marks a watershed, when the conflict passes beyond immediate consciousness, past a memory of fathers and grandfathers, and grows increasingly remote.

There is a duty and a compulsion to keep these voices alive. Whether Tommy Atkins was a 'lion' led by 'donkeys' or whether the generals were thwarted by advances in technology that rendered a well-held trench line unbreakable is not the subject of this book. Arthur Roberts was not just a military figure: his life is a window on the twentieth century. He was of mixed race, yet he remained in education till the age of 18 – an achievement in itself. His grasp of language and grammar were exemplary and he was as skilled with the brush as the pen. His war memoir is fluent and accomplished, delivered with humour and panache, yet this is but part of a wholly remarkable story.

Arthur suffered recurring foot problems and may not have seen further active service after 1917. He was demobbed on 5 December 1919.

By now Glasgow was his home city and that was where he would finish his apprenticeship. He returned to sketching, was confirmed into the Anglican faith and resumed his interest in music, particularly the banjo. He met his future wife in the 1930s, though they did not actually marry until many years later. He continued to live and work in Glasgow during the Second World War, though whether he ever joined the Home Guard or Civil Defence Corps remains unclear. His post-war photos show him as still very much the dandy, even on the beach! His wife Jessie died young, aged only 63. His next relationship, with Jessie's cousin Jean McDonald, lasted until she too died in 1977. Arthur's health declined and his later years were spent in care, where he died at the age of 84.

The house in Mount Vernon had been the property of an elderly widower who never got round to clearing the attic: it lay undisturbed for decades. The new buyers knew nothing of Arthur William David Roberts until the day they came across that large cardboard box with its wealth of memorabilia. Twenty years had passed since Arthur's death. Gazing on the life story laid out on the attic floor, it seemed as though Arthur had prepared his hoard and left its discovery to chance.

His Great War diary and collected memoirs had been boxed up with his satchel, official documents placed separately. Photos, postcards and drawings together with three albums, various Christmas cards and other, unrelated items, all lay waiting for their audience. The young woman, Laura, who, with her partner Murray, had bought the house, used some of the Great War material in her academic work. It was her course tutor who advised her to consult a military expert. That was when the full significance of the diary emerged. Morag and Roy, who had agreed to take on the research task, consulted Ian Martin at the KOSB Museum in Berwick-upon-Tweed. Thanks to Ian's experience and diligence a clearer record of Arthur's Great War service came to light. Morag and Roy were now fully possessed by historical fever – they had to know more.

How had the box ended up in this particular attic? Arthur appeared to have had no connection with the address. A series of clues emerged from the cache of personal records. Tellingly, his death certificate (dated 15 January 1982) listed his executor as a Mr J. Walker. He was the elderly widower who had owned the property – the link was now established.

Ian Martin, at the KOSB Museum, put Morag and Roy in touch with two historians who were researching Great War material. Like Morag and Roy, Rosie Serdiville and John Sadler were hooked as soon as they read Arthur's diary – this book had to be written.

The diary, reminiscences and memoirs provoked considerable media interest worldwide in 2011. Press coverage prompted TV features and the story of Arthur Roberts jumped from obscurity to near celebrity. People began to get in touch. Doreen Thomas was a distant cousin of Arthur's and still lived in Bristol. Another cousin, Darryl Gwynne, made contact from Georgetown, Canada. Two important local witnesses – James Wilson, who'd been Arthur's apprentice in Duncan Stewart & Co. and Allison O'Neill, latterly his key care worker, in Crookston Care Home – were inspired to come forward. This book represents a distillation of the available evidence from the above sources, and we are deeply grateful to all of them for enhancing our knowledge and understanding of this remarkable man.

This, then, is the story of a man's life, a man who was at once both extraordinary and commonplace. Arthur Roberts comes alive through his own words: erudite, confident and witty. He gives himself to us as a man of his times, an adopted Glaswegian, his life a window on the life of this great city through much of the twentieth century. Those who seek evidence of racism and discrimination will be disappointed. Arthur's ethnicity is never of concern to him, and his only reference to it is in terms of his army service. To Arthur, Glasgow appeared a cosmopolitan and tolerant place. That he does not report any tensions may come as a surprise to some readers. Arthur is the medium, Glasgow and the unfolding of the twentieth century is his canvas.

1

THE BOY

Life can be hard for incomers. Later in this book we refer to the Race Riots of 1919 when Glasgow, like so many other cities, erupted into violence. Fuelled by economic desperation and community distrust, groups of white and black seamen clashed around the docks. On the surface it appeared there was scant welcome in this city for a man of colour.

The experience of Arthur William David Roberts proved different. He was not a native Glaswegian, having been born in Bristol on 28 April 1897. His father, David Roberts Jenkins, was Afro-Caribbean, his mother, Laura Roberts Jenkins (née Dann), was a West Country lass. David Roberts (he dropped 'Jenkins' before Arthur was born) worked as a ship's steward (at one time on the SS *Micmac*). Arthur was still very young when he and his father moved 400 miles north to Glasgow, the 'Second City of the Empire'. They would settle in the Anderston district:

The suburb adjoins the western extremity of Argyle Street and stood quite apart from Glasgow till about 1830. Later it communicated with Glasgow by an open thoroughfare, called Anderston Walk. [In Arthur's time it was completely enveloped in the western extensions of Glasgow.] It stood amidst these extensions with old dingy features of its own, in strong contrast to the surrounding impressive Victorian architecture: impinging on the Clyde along what in the early 1900s was a dense and very busy part of the old docks, but what formerly lay far westward beyond the old dockland's lower extremity: at its centre an old main street, Stobcross Street, deflecting at an acute angle from Argyle Street, leading on toward Finniston. Here there were a number of narrow old streets very densely peopled, and a number of newer or more airy ones, mostly going parallel with one another, at right angles to Stobcross Street, to the Clyde. This area is now unrecognisable due to the construction of the Kingston Bridge in the late 1960s.[1]

This rather dry portrait describes a period of profound change and rapid growth. From long centuries of semi-rural calm the area had sprung into industrialised life during the second half of the nineteenth century. The brash new industries of the great city, shipbuilding, iron-founding, engineering, their growth fuelled by proximity to the packed waterside, spurred a demand for mass housing. Tenements were thrown up to house the influx, densely packed with a slew of new churches to feed the spiritual needs of this burgeoning population. Two vast municipal-style bakeries provided further employment. Alongside these larger concerns many small backstreet workshops flourished.

Immigration was nothing new in Glasgow. During the late eighteenth and early nineteenth century a rush of Irish Protestants were drawn by opportunities in the booming textile trade, their Catholic countrymen attracted by a rising demand for unskilled labourers. These two communities had a history of enmity and carried their prejudices with them. About the time Arthur's family shifted into Anderston, a fresh wave of immigrants, this time escaping from agricultural stagnation in Italy, began to arrive in Scotland with Glasgow as their main destination. The city became a vast cosmopolitan sprawl. New wealth and confidence fuelled a rash of major civic projects – the Loch Katrine Aqueduct, City Subway and Tramway, City Chambers, Mitchell Library and Kelvingrove Museum all owe their origin to this period. The population had long since surpassed that of Edinburgh – Glasgow became one of the first cities in Europe to house more than a million inhabitants. Major international exhibitions were staged at Kelvingrove in 1888, 1901 and 1911.

This urbane and confident facade hid a darker reality of slums and poverty, of hunger and disease, high infant mortality and reduced life expectancy due to squalor and want. Black immigrants faced an even darker time, as reported in the *Scotsman* in 2007 (200th anniversary of the abolition of the slave trade in the British Empire):

John Glassford was a hugely successful tobacco merchant who had a street named after him. It is near Buchanan Street, named after another tobacco merchant. Jamaica and Virginia Streets also attest to Glasgow's connections with tobacco and slavery. These streets crisscross modern-day Glasgow like scars from a slave-master's lash.

In Glasgow, the city's slave history is only half-hidden. Massive signs announcing Merchant City adorn George Square, and the Glasgow Museum of Modern Art – one of the city's most prominent structures – is now housed in what was once a tobacco merchant's private residence. What is missing in these edifices are the appalling conditions that brought this splendour into being. The Barons that built Glasgow into what it is today made their money from trade with slave-worked plantations. This trade was vital to the plantations' survival and so to slavery itself.[2]

A series of industries boomed in Glasgow as a result of the trade in sugar, tobacco and later cotton – rope and leather works, iron foundries, textile factories churning out clothes for slaves – the wealth spilled out through the region.

When the young Arthur Roberts and his father relocated to Glasgow they would know very little of this. Why they chose Glasgow is not recorded. The reason was probably family related. Throughout the course of his diary and reminiscences Arthur rarely refers to any form of bigotry or discrimination. This is not to say he was never on the receiving end of racism, but he certainly does not see himself cast in the role of victim. Throughout, he appears confident, even buoyant, at ease within his own frame. He never appears to have contemplated living anywhere other than Glasgow, which he clearly regarded throughout his life as home. His childhood was spent in the sprawling, smoke-laden labyrinth of Anderston, one working family among many. The dark, austere tenements resonated with the clamour of industry and trade – redolent with the fumes of leather, oil, steam, sweat and a hundred varieties of cooking and spilling ale houses. These crowded tenements housed commerce on the ground floor, split by narrow alleys or 'closes' giving access to an internal yard. Rear stairs led to individual households above. Each household – either a single room or a room and kitchen – typically housed an extended family. Arthur would do his growing up in this intensely communal setting, one that produced a fair measure of local pride and assurance, coupled with deprivation, chronic health problems, dank, dismal and perennially overcrowded. Arthur slept in a cubicle in a model lodging house called the Exhibition Hotel but presumably spent meal times and leisure hours in the single-end at 635 Argyle Street.

He began his education at Finniston Primary before moving to senior school at Kent Road. At this time the University of Glasgow was at the forefront of learning innovation, educating the rising bourgeoisie for careers in business and the professions. The school-leaving age had been raised to 14 in 1901. From the 1870s Scotland had begun moving toward a system of universal state-funded education, compulsory for all 5 to 13-year-olds. Larger urban school boards established 'Higher Grade' (Secondary) schools, such as that which Arthur would attend, as a cheaper alternative to the burgh schools. The Scottish Education Department introduced a Leaving Certificate Examination in 1888 to set national standards for secondary education and in 1890 school fees were abolished.

As he walked daily along crowded streets to school, Arthur would have witnessed the spectacle of small herds of bleating sheep and nervous cattle being driven through the streets. Granite setts ringing with the clopping of cloven hooves, pigs were hustled noisily towards their final destination at Sir Thomas Lipton's original store at 101 Stobcross Street. These animals were moving adverts for the enterprising grocer, their fat necks slung with prominent notices proclaiming: 'I'm on my way to Lipton's, the best place in town for bacon!'

Harry Lauder was the doyen of innumerable variety theatres, but the suffragette leader Mrs Pankhurst was a more contentious visitor. Arthur's higher grade school at Kent Road was scarcely 200yd from St Andrew's Hall where, on the evening of 11 March 1914, a suffragette meeting degenerated into a brawl, with Glasgow's finest being pelted with plant holders and a few blank rounds discharged. Undeterred by the heated reception, Mrs Pankhurst was duly dragged off into incarceration – prompting a march by some 4,000 protesters.

Arthur was a bright and studious boy. Lively but conscientious, he showed an early talent for drawing and his sketches soon became proficient. He was by nature sociable and gregarious, in many ways a born actor. Joining the Boy Scouts suited his orderly temperament and the crisp uniform was an obvious attraction for the emerging dandy. Music, particularly, at this time, the bugle, proved an added impulse. The need for practice must have been something of a strain for those round him in such densely crowded conditions!

1914 saw storm clouds gathering over Europe. Arthur and his emerging generation could have no idea of the Calvary that was awaiting them. On 28 June, in the Balkan city of Sarajevo, a teen assassin fired two fatal shots that would change the world forever. This storm had been brewing for over forty years, since Bismarck's plans had first included the humiliation of France and ushered in an era of nervous yet aggressive superpowers divided into armed camps, poised to mobilise. Glasgow was one of the world's greatest industrial centres and Scotland was about to be precipitated into the world's first industrial war – conflict on a scale and of an intensity never before dreamed of. The optimistic shout at war's outset 'It will all be over by Christmas' would ring as hollow as the claim, at war's end, that veterans would return to 'a land fit for heroes'.

It has been said, not without truth, that Britain fielded four armies during the Great War. First, the original regular army and reserves that formed the British Expeditionary Force (BEF) in 1914 (immortalised as 'the Old Contemptibles'). Second, the Territorial Battalions, third Kitchener's New Army Battalions and, finally, the conscript army of 1917–18. The core tactical unit throughout was the battalion (typically 750–1,000 men). This was headed by a colonel, essentially an honorary position, but actual day-to-day command was vested in the lieutenant-colonel. As a rough rule, some 10 per cent of battalion strength was kept in reserve, left out of the battle ('LOOB'), as a core around which to rebuild if the unit was badly cut up. All too often this pragmatic prophecy would indeed come to pass. Below lieutenant-colonel was the major, who normally commanded the 250-strong HQ Company. Then 'A', 'B', 'C' and 'D' Companies were each commanded by captains, all at similar notional strength. Each company was then divided into four sub-units or platoons: an HQ platoon (commanded by a lieutenant with an NCO and four privates or 'riflemen' in a Rifle unit); then four other platoons, numbered 1–4, led usually by a second-lieutenant (subaltern), with four NCOs and thirty-two privates. The platoon itself was broken down into sections, the smallest tactical unit, each of eight men and an NCO. Crucially, the infantry battalion in 1914 possessed only two Vickers medium machine guns. From 1915 firepower was significantly enhanced by the introduction of lighter automatic weapons, such as the Lewis Gun. Latterly, the medium machine-gunners were transferred to the Machine Gun Corps and the number of Lewis guns available was increased from four per battalion to four times that number and double that again after the Somme. In 1914, four battalions, under a brigadier-general, formed a brigade and three brigades a division. This larger unit was commanded by a major-general and possessed its own signallers, medical staff, engineers and gunners. Some three, perhaps four, divisions would be formed into an army corps, led this time by a lieutenant-general. A number of corps, say four–six, would constitute an 'army'. Britain would have five armies deployed on the Western Front with total ration strength of over a million men.

The young Arthur Roberts, like so many of his generation, had a taste for the pomp of war; his keenness for the plangent notes of the bugle would echo through his military service:

During my school days I was possessed of great military inclinations. Anything in the form of drill, or manoeuvres, interested me exceedingly. As a result when the church to which I belonged, got a troop of scouts, I worried my father so much for permission to join them, that at last, for relief he consented. To cut a long story short, I took this good opportunity of learning the bugle, and speaking frankly I became fairly efficient at the instrument. Some years later, the Great War broke out, and in the course of time I was with many thousands more engulfed in that titanic conflict. As will be seen in the diary, I was one time stationed at Le Havre, and it was here, that, the following incident took place.

The bugler of the camp in which I was, became very friendly with me, so me, fancying my prowess as a bugler, it was only natural I should ask him to let me blow a call. Oh how I have reason to regret that request, and if I could only have seen twelve short days ahead of me! Looking at it from another point, it just had to be, so there is no use worrying now. However, to return to the story, he complied and I blew that particular call in fine style, much to my satisfaction and his surprise. This, dear reader was the first move of fate in the game. Follow closely. Now, unless there are two or more buglers in a camp, the chap who has the job, is practically tied to his post. Imagine the joy of this bugler discovering me. Believe me; he made full use of his discovery. Any night he was other-wise engaged, I acted as his deputy with pleasure. Thus, fate made its second move.

It so happened, the bugler was sweating on the top line for leave, about this time, so I was not surprised when, 21st December 1917 to be exact, he informed me gleefully; he had been warned for leave. The orderly sergeant promptly told me off for bugler, for the ensuing fifteen days, being as he said (bunkum of course) the only man in the camp able for the job. This was move the third. How mysterious are the ways of fate. Watch how magnificently it works up to its final blow.

No doubt, it was a cushy job, for it entailed no such distasteful things as work or inspections, or guards and such like. To tell the truth, the job was too alluring, no wonder I was elated. I was looking forward to fifteen glorious days, so, as it was pay-day, why should I not find enjoyment suitable to my mood? No sooner thought than did. I had a glorious time (curtain). Isn't fate playing well?

Curiously enough, the officer's servants and cooks, amalgamated that same night. Their movements after leaving camp were unknown to any, but themselves, but fortune smiles on the Bacchanalians at times, so they successfully, like myself, evaded the maw, of the ever ready red-caps, and the wee small hours witnessed their straggling return. Of course, I'm only imagining that they straggled. Here we find fate has made its fifth move and is now ready, with all the heroes, and the super hero (me), lying drunk, incapable, and happy for the grand finale.

Oh dear reader! Have you ever tried to write, with truth and candour about one of your own personal disasters? If you would be advised – don't. I took up this work before I knew, so it's the hand on the plough business. I'm afraid I'm guilty of straying again, but here goes for the great smash. From a dreamless sleep, I was boisterously wakened to find myself half out of bed, and the orderly man yelling 'Hi! Hi! It's after six o'clock. Get Up! Get Up! Man, you're the bugler, your late, come on! Get up!'

When I recovered some of my senses, I attempted to rise, but instead, I rolled out of bed. 'What! What!' says I, my mouth like a sewage pipe, 'where's the damn bugle, where's my trousers and my boots? What time is it? Screw on the lights somebody. Oh hell, this is clink for me this time. Damn the rotten bugle. Where's the mouth piece?' I found the trousers, but no boots, although I discovered my socks. By this time, I was delaying myself by hurrying too fast. The time was flying, so I followed its example. With only my shirt and trousers and socks on, I dashed out into the December air, with my eyes half shut, and before I stopped, the bugle was up and I was blowing like a hero in action. It was now 6.20 a.m. but the call was over, so I came flopping back, imagine me flopping, to smarten myself up a bit. Dear reader, leave me to go on flopping and take a peep into the officer's quarters.

Everything is hustle and bustle; the cooks are poking fires, while the waiters are setting tables and dressing themselves at the same time. Oh Heavens! Why didn't somebody remain sober and look after the officer's dinner. There's the dinner call, and devil the dinner's ready. By gum, the guard-room will be well filled directly. With matters in such a deplorable state, I must drag you away gentle one.

I had now flopped as far as the door of my hut, but guess my surprise when I saw the boys lying rocking in their beds laughing like to split themselves. When they saw me they roared and shrieked and kicked, 'What's up?' says I. This was like putting a match to gun-powder. The chaps rolled, tumbled, choked and spluttered with merriment. Similar sounds were borne to my ears from other huts. 'Tell me the joke I roared, I don't look as bad as all that.'

At last somebody stuttered, 'Ha! Ha! Well done! Ha! Ha! You idiot! Haw! Haw! Haw! You're drunk yet! He! He! That was Ha! Ha! The Officer's Mess He! He! You sounded! Haw! Haw! Haw!'

'What!' I screamed. 'My God, that's my leave gone west now, oh Heavens! I'll never go out again in a good mood.' I don't think there was one man able to stand erect, on parade, that morning for laughing.

By the way it was well for me that I was lying in the guard-room that day, or the officer servants would have scalped me. They had risen from a drunken sleep, hearing the dinner call, proceeded to prepare dinner, instead of breakfast. Such was the final move of fate in that game and its completeness leaves no room for improvement.

Notes

1. In 1882–84, Frances Groome's *Ordnance Gazetteer of Scotland*, 1882–84, cited on www.visionofbritain.org.uk/place/20164.
2. The *Scotsman*, 20 March 2007.

2

THE RECRUIT

Duddingston Camp,
Portobello,
Midlothian,
Dear Aunt, March 1917

I have thoroughly recovered my health and am progressing finely. The order for us to go to Musselborough has been cancelled so we shall be staying on here. I hope you are drawing the half pay alright. I suppose the old boy would be kicking up a dust about me but just let him talk till he is tired then he'll dry up. Tell Lily to look after my pet tie-pin because when I come home from the front I shall be looking for it.

Don't forget to let me know when Lily's wedding takes place so that I can get drunk here and imagine that I'm at it. I've to be inoculated again so again I shall be laid up if I'm not laid down. Tell all friends I was asking for them.

If you or Lily could spare time you might please make me a little cake. Say about a pound or half-a-pound. It won't cost much and it's very seldom we get what you would call really good cake here. I've seen two or three drafts going away since I've been here and it feels so funny while the men are passing.

The bands are playing good-oh and you feel as if you were going too but when one sees the mothers and sisters and sweethearts crying as they keep step with their loved ones and the fathers walking silent with eyes red and shining with unshed tears it makes one feel creepy especially when the big drum booms and the kettle drums roll but somebody must go.

In the draft that went away today there were three men taken out from the guard room, that's our prison, handcuffed and marched off to France without being able to shake hands with some of their friends who were waiting on them at the gate. I hope when I go that I'll be able to walk as straight as any man in the draft.

I hope you and Lily are in good health and that you are not both suffering from those attacks of headaches.

I think I have said all that I can say just now so I will close and retire.

Wishing you and Lily the best of health and that you practice economy.

I remain your loving nephew
Arthur Roberts.

The opening battles, in which the BEF was pitched against enormous odds, were fought at Mons and Le Cateau in a fast-moving war of manoeuvre, quite unlike the stalemate that set in during the autumn of 1914. Wrong-footed and exposed, the BEF fought some masterly, if costly, actions and played its part in General Joffre's counterstroke on the Marne. From there it advanced into Belgium in what would become known as 'the Race for the Sea', which ended in the ferocity of First Ypres in October. This battle and those of 1915 drastically reduced the ranks of regular formations and handed the baton, in part, to Kitchener's 'New Service' Battalions.

After stalemate in 1915 came the colossal slaughter at Verdun and then the Somme, a battle which cost Britain and the Empire more dead than the entire course of the Second World War. In 1917 the British learned how to crack the linear German defences and scored some great successes before German resilience and new defensive systems drowned all hopes in Flanders mud. For spring 1918, the Kaiser's generals unleashed a series of blistering offensives that came close to breaking the Allies. Close but not close enough and the tide inexorably turned, the victory won at enormous cost.

We have said that Britain fielded four distinct armies in the course of the war. First the regulars and reservists, the 'Old Contemptibles' of fame, next the Territorial Battalions, formed from the rump of militia and yeomanry by Haldane in 1908. After them were Kitchener's New Army units, formed from that titanic rush to volunteer when young men thought war was a great adventure, born from the great man's unjustified disdain for Territorials. Lastly, limping in the wake of these eviscerated volunteers, were the conscripts who began to filter into the ranks during 1917–18, a very different type of unwilling warrior, proof of a desperate need to maintain the line in the face of terrible losses. This would not be war as their ancestors had known it, rippling platoon volleys in open fields with battles decided in an hour. This would be a grinding, bloodied attrition of static trenches, battles that dragged on for month after frenzied month, consuming flesh and bone in prodigious quantities.

By the time war broke out in 1914, the Scottish Territorials numbered just over 50,000. Their training and general state of readiness was so finely pitched that the War Office was confident the battalions would agree to serve overseas if called upon. The Territorials were only obliged to serve on any home front; deployment across the Channel required volunteering. The authorities would not be disappointed. At the outset, Scots comprised only some 8 per cent of the regulars, but during the four long years of conflict some 557,618 men enlisted, over 40 per cent of the nation's young adult males, and they formed six full divisions. The Scottish National War Memorial at Edinburgh Castle lists a total of 147,647 fatal casualties. This means that roughly a quarter of those young men were killed. The Royal Scots alone fielded thirty-five battalions and lost 11,000 dead. Scotland suffered more than any other combatant nation and paid a very high price for the peerless reputation of her fighting men. Arthur Roberts was one of these.

Arthur first enlisted in 3rd Battalion King's Own Scottish Borderers on 13 February 1917, but was then transferred to 2nd Battalion Royal Scots Fusiliers on 3 June 1917, the unit which would be his home for all of his active war service. The diary covers the period from 19 May 1917 to 6 March 1918, and says little about recruitment and basic training. His carefully posed photographs from both of these famous regiments show his penchant for style. Most young recruits of the period seem stiff and ill at ease in their shapeless khaki, posing for the camera an alien and rather alarming experience. This is not the case with Arthur – his uniforms fit so well as to seem tailored, and he wears them with the aplomb of an actor – more Beau Geste than Tommy Atkins.

The Royal Scots Fusiliers (RSF) was a famous regiment, raised in Scotland in 1678 by Charles Erskine, de jure 5th Earl of Mar, for service against contentious covenanters during the Second Whig Revolt (1678–79), deployed to keep the peace and suppress brigands, caterans and rebels. During the Glorious Revolution of 1688 the regiment was ordered south and while, at the outset, its members remained loyal to the Stewart James II, like most they swapped to serve William of Orange when James fled. The regiment, like so many others, later fought against the Jacobites at Culloden. A long roll of battle honours followed and some eighteen battalions served during the Great War. Lord Trenchard, father of the RAF, had served during the South African War. One of his opponents was Deneys Reitz, future South African prime minister, a former Boer Commando leader, but who, from 1914, commanded the 1st Battalion.

For Sir Douglas Haig, 1917 would not prove to be a vintage year. Russia would collapse and French armies, as though infected by the same discordant virus, in many cases refused to fight, at least on the offensive. Italy would be hammered at Caporetto and attempts in the Middle East to break the deadlock against 'Johnny Turk' in Gaza met with scant success. Haig's offensive at Arras and Vimy achieved wonders at the outset, though the former swiftly degenerated into yet another costly battle of attrition. General Plumer and the Second Army performed tremendous feats at Messines but then Haig's great summer offensive, the Third Battle of Ypres (popularly known by the name of one of its objectives, Passchendaele) became the very symbol of fruitless slaughter in a hellish sea of mud.

On 16 April, French General Robert Nivelle's great offensive – desperately flawed and pressed home with the frenzy of self-delusion – commenced. For their general's folly, the *Poilus* paid a fearful blood-price. Undeterred, Nivelle pushed on, casting blame on every head but his own. These failed attacks cost another 100,000 casualties. For many in the line this was simply too much. On 29 April, the murmurs of discontent hardened into outright refusal.

On 9 April, Haig had attacked at Arras. This was essentially a large-scale diversion intended to keep German reserves pinned in that sector while Nivelle's master plan unfolded. On the first day the Canadian Corps, fighting as a single cohesive force for the first time, performed magnificently and took Vimy Ridge. This seemingly impregnable bastion had bloodily defied all Allied attempts for the preceding three years. Allenby's Third Army made astonishing progress on the first day at Arras. But despite the vastly improved bombardment and deep penetrations, the British could not capitalise on this initial success. The Germans, resilient as ever, recovered their breath and stood their ground. The battle went grinding on, the same weary and bloody toll of attrition, Allenby losing over 4,000 men a day till further attacks were finally called off on 17 May.

Despite the success at Messines, there was no immediate follow-up and Crown Prince Rupprecht of Bavaria, commanding German forces in Flanders, was given time to take in the lessons of Messines and strengthen his line accordingly. He was advised by Colonel Fritz von Lossberg, the 'Vauban' of trench warfare. He now created a series of grid fortifications studded with redoubts and fronted by a deep but thinly held outpost line, manned primarily by machine-gunners sheltering in blockhouses or ruined farms. These, the elite of the German Army, promised to exact a high toll on any attacker before the main line was ever reached. As John Buchan, in his short history of the RSF, records:

Von Armin having learned the lesson of his defeat at Messines, had prepared his defences. The nature of the ground did not permit of a second Hindenburg Line, since deep dugouts and concreted trenches were impossible because of the waterlogged soil. He was compelled to find new tactics, and his solution was the 'pill-box'. These were small concrete forts, sited amongst the ruins of a farm or in some derelict piece of woodland, often raised by only a yard or two above the ground level and bristling with machine-guns. They were echeloned in depth with great skill, and in the wiring, alleys were left so and [*sic*] unwary advance would be entrapped among them and exposed to enfilading fire. Their small size made them a difficult mark for heavy guns, and, since they were protected by concrete at least three feet thick, they were impregnable to the ordinary field-artillery barrage.

The enemy's plan was to hold his first line – which was often a mere string of shall craters – with few men, who would fall back before an assault. He had his guns well behind, so that they would not be captured in the first rush, and would be available for a barrage if his opponents became entangled in the pill-box zone. Any attack would be permitted to make some advance but, if the German plan worked well, that advance would be short lived and it would be dearly paid for. Instead of the cast-iron front of the Hindenburg Line, the Flanders line would be highly elastic, but it would spring back into position after pressure with a deadly rebound.[1]

Arthur Roberts would be one of those who found out first-hand just how formidable the Flanders line would prove. Like most of those who would find themselves at the 'sharp end' this young Tommy was more preoccupied with the day-to-day:

In the preface of my diary, it will be noted, that I have stated, that many sad stories and laughable incidents, could be extracted from between the lines of that book. Naturally, in the diary of any person of limited time, and sparingly equipped with writing material, a small phrase may, and generally does, cover a very pathetic, amusing, or hair raising experience. This statement will be fully observed in all its significance, if the diary is referred to, whilst perusing this work. Lastly, for my own tranquility of conscience it will be needless for me to say, that the incidents related are true, and personal experiences.

We need to sound a note of caution at this point. Soldiers' diaries are a day-to-day account. The reader who expects fire and smoke, dust and glory on each page is apt to be disappointed. War is largely about spit and polish, discomfort and waiting. During many long spells the greatest hazard was boredom. But the Western Front, like a sleeping dragon, was always waiting, ready to stir, belch fire and drag yet more into its dark, infernal coils:

> Saturday 19 May 1917: At last I have started on my way to the front. The draft left mid great excitement and playing of bands – Major Harris was crying on the platform as he waved his handkerchief. I am now trying to write this in the train. I wondered as I left Edinburgh if I should ever see it again.

One of Marlborough's redcoats toiling on the road to Blenheim in 1704 would have had little or no difficulty in recognising his great-grandson marching in the rain towards the ridge of Mont St Jean under Wellington over a century later. Both wore the famous red coat. They marched or rode as armies had through distant centuries. They wheeled and drilled, delivered their platoon volleys in a very similar manner. Both carried a smooth-bore flintlock musket that might just kill their man at fifty yards. Yet Wellington's infantryman – *that article*, as his commander described him – might have found far greater difficulty in rec-ognising his own great-grandson, slogging along the hot pave towards Mons in 1914. *Tommy* was clad in stiff khaki. He carried the SMLE bolt-action repeating rifle, deadly at a dozen times the distance of its predecessor. Much of his travel was under-taken by rail and the ubiquitous tin meant he could fight all year round and still be fed. None of this promised an easier life. Indeed his would very likely be harder, more terrifying and very much shorter:

> Sunday 20 May 1917: We landed safely in France (from Folkestone) about 9.45 a.m. from the ship *Princess Victoria*. The draft marched through Boulogne to the rest camp (St Martin's), situated about a mile behind the town and on a steep hill. I was put on fire piquet about 2.30 p.m. till 5.30 p.m.

We retired at 9 p.m. after roll call. I am looking forward to the long march to Étaples tomorrow with dread.

New small arms, accurate and deadly, were not the only lethal hazards on the battlefield. Field guns were quick firers, throwing high-explosive shells over long distances with fearful accuracy. Hiram Maxim had heeded a colleague's exhortation that, if he wanted to make money, he should invent a means whereby European armies could slaughter each other with greater ease. He obliged and the machine-gun, with a range of 2,000yd and a rate of fire of some 600 rounds per minute, would change the nature of the battlefield forever.

Young men enlisted for a wide variety of reasons. At the outset many were swept away in the flood of patriotic sentiment. By 1917 – with casualty lists soaring to undreamt of levels and the vast char-nel of the Somme behind – illusions could not be sustained. Britain was unique in that she had fought the war using only volunteers, but conscription had to be introduced in 1916. The enthusiasts of 1914 were mostly bled out. For Arthur Roberts, like so many others, war offered a raft of novel experiences, not all disagreeable. Few had travelled very far; fewer still had ever crossed the Channel. Many had only had limited contact with the other sex. For all its celibate promise, the army recognised the need for distractions:

It never has been my intention, that this book should be one of an ideal man's actions during a military period of his life. In order therefore to immediately dispel any cause for surprise which you may be inclined to experience, I must here and now be frank, and tell you that I am not, nor was, at the time of which I write, an ideal person. My actions here related there-fore, also lack the ideals. I have said I will be frank and frank I shall be if I am to be able to let this book be read, and to con-scientiously say this is a book of facts. It is no object or wish of mine, in constructing this work to gain praise for myself as a soldier, or notoriety as a gay-spark, but I maintain that in a work of this kind, the indiscreet should be related with the otherwise. If that is not done then the reader is allowed to gain a false impression or an ample field for surmising is left open. However for better or for worse here goes for the yarn.

I shall never forget my introduction night to a red lamp. It was shortly after my arrival in Le Havre. It came about this way, one night some of the boys and myself were sitting round a blazing stove in our hut, gossiping as soldiers, like women will, and the subject was about the best places of entertainment and refreshment in the town. By the way our camp was about a mile and a quarter from the nearest car terminus. During the talk, I found that there were more ways of enjoyment than I had been used to, hitherto, my night outs had consisted of going into a café to eat, and drink, and sing, until I could eat, drink, and sing no more.

What we now prissily refer to as 'the sex industry' was enjoying something of a boom between the years 1914–18. Many French and Belgians suffered terribly as a consequence of the conflict, others, away from the front, saw business opportunities on a biblical scale. The BEF with its tens of thousands of fit, testosterone-charged young men, had many requirements:

Most of the cafés up the line had no accommodation for side-shows, and besides money could be made quicker by selling drinks and eatables. Variation is one of the spices of life. I always like to talk from experience, but like in making a dumpling too much spice is not good. However the upshot of our gossip resulted in me resolving to go to town to see for myself. Unfortunately that week was the blank week, in other words not pay-week. We were paid fortnightly, never the less I would make this a reconnoitering expedition, and then wouldn't I make the fur fly on the following week.

Now in the army, Sunday is only strictly held during church parade, after the parade the order of the day is 'into bed or out of barracks'. There being no further parades on this day of the week, this programme is a very practicable one, as a consequence therefore, the Sabbath day is monopolised by the troops for excursions, or exploration purposes. As will be seen in the diary, the 30th December 1917 was the day chosen by me for my search for experience.

Although I was dutifully lined up with the parade that morning, I don't think a very religious heart beat beneath the polished button of my left breast pocket, and they were not solemn thoughts that buzzed about under the tassel of my Balmoral Bonnet. Anyhow as far as that section of the army was concerned, a certain number of men with boots and buttons polished, and chins shaved, were required on parade and I was one of them, I was present so everything was satisfactory.

After dinner, I gave myself a final brush up, buckled on my square pushing belt, and swaggered out of camp like a new toy soldier from a toy box. The walk to the car put me in good form, and by the time I dismounted at the Hotel de Ville, I thought the only thing I needed to give me a distinguished appearance was a curly moustache. With the confidence of a person who knows he is faultlessly attired, I leisurely, with the correct military stiffness in my back, made my way up the busy shopping centre known as the Rue de Paris.

I was certainly fortunate this day, for I had not proceeded far when I ran into one of my hut mates. There and then we made hasty arrangements for a sightseeing visit to the fast quarter. We walked to the end of the Rue de Paris, and turning to the left we were on the Quay de Southampton. About two streets were passed on the Quay side when a third was

reached by name of the Rue de Gallions. 'Here we are,' said
my escort, as we turned into this thoroughfare and instinctively I tightened my belt.

Brothels were a recognised feature on both sides of the line. It
was inevitable when the armies were locked in this terrible, lingering embrace of death across no-man's-land that such comfort
would not only be provided by enterprising locals but would be
accepted by the high command. As befitted the class distinctions
between officers and men, the former attended the 'blue lamp'
establishments and the latter the 'red'. Levels of sophistication at
the former were generally a good deal higher, conforming more
to the Edwardian model of a high-class establishment, while
other ranks were obliged to accept 'economy class', varying from
basic to totally squalid:

> It was a curious kind of street, for the distance of about twenty
> yards it was practically a lane, then it suddenly opened out
> into a fairly wide but short street. This wide portion was about
> eighty yards in length, as far as I can recollect, then on one
> side, a building jutted out bringing the street again into the
> category of a lane. At this time of the year, the evenings draw
> in very quickly, and although it was only about four o'clock
> when we arrived, the lights were blazing from every door,
> window, and fanciful glass sign. Most portals had an attractive
> glass fanlight with the number in the centre of it.
>
> Every door-way was brightly illuminated and the inner
> doors and partitions were decorated with stained glass and
> brass knobs, and plates, and rails, well polished and glittering
> in the electric light. At each opening on an old box, or rickety
> chair, there generally sat an old crone, who showered knowing
> winks and sly smiles on the patrons of her particular employer,
> and promises of luring entertainments and refreshments to be

had within to those who hesitated, or were inclined to try the next place. The windows of these places were of fairly big dimensions, and were usually of stained glass, but in almost every case here they were at least six feet from the ground.

I think there were three cafés on each side of the wide part of the street, while in the narrow part of the further end, were I believe two small cafés.

One of the first things I observed on entering the street was that nearly everybody moving about it was in British uniform. This fact made me feel that I was not moving about entirely among strangers. What completed this feeling was the knowledge that I was still under the disciplinary hand of the army, for along the centre of the street with service revolvers shewing prominently, slowly placed [*sic*] two red-caps.

As I have already stated this was our blind week, and money was scarce, so my guide thought that I should first see the inside of a small café, and then I should not be so bewildered or shocked when I visited the more class cafés of the same game. I won't describe our visit to this inferior place, because I can save time and space, and give the reader a better idea of these kind of resorts by detailing one of the big, full-blast, gilt-edged cafés. Suffice it to say that the visit was certainly a startler to me, and it whetted my appetite for further knowledge, which I was determined to gain at the earliest opportunity. I had not the golden key however, so I had to retain my impatience for another seven days.

Senior officers were prepared to overlook the more obvious moral questions in the belief that soldiers, particularly married men, needed regular sexual release to maintain fighting spirit. Principles took second place to pragmatism. It was only Kitchener himself who took a dim view of such apparent licentiousness. He held that the men should not fraternise in any way with local women, they should even avoid conversation. Given very few spoke French and a crude phrasebook was yet to be issued, this was not a major difficulty!

I have described the outside aspects of the Rue de Gallions in general, it now shall be my aim to portray to the reader, the mode of conduct and the inside appearances of the people and buildings, of the street.

On Sunday, 6th January 1918, exactly seven days later, my pal and I were once more turning into the Rue de Gallions, with our boots, and buttons, polished and our cap badges bidding defiance to the world. We strode along like conquering heroes entering a captured citadel, and we felt like such; for had we not the golden key and were we not going to wrest the knowledge from these buildings with the bright lights and fancy entrances? Certainly we were confident of the success of our undertaking. Halting for a moment, and taking a survey of our surroundings from the inside end of the lane, we selected one of the café's [*sic*] for our visit, the second on the left I remember, and ignoring the old crone outside the first café, we passed on and entered our choice.

My pal led the way, and pushing open one of the much ornamented doors, I followed on his heels. Outside many subdued and various sounds of revelry had been heard by us, but as we entered the door, it seemed to me as if I had walked into a gigantic musical box. For a moment I was dazzled by the lights and reflections of mirrors, and brass ornamentations, and I had certainly been nonplussed by this sudden entry into this haunt of the libertine, so that it was more mechanically than otherwise, that I followed my chum to a table. My observation faculties gradually returned to me, and the jumbled mass of people, lights, reflections, glasses and furniture and a hundred and one things that go to make up a cabaret commenced to sort themselves out in my temporarily dulled mind.

I assented to a drink, which my pal proposed, and he noticing my embarrassment offered me his case. We lit up, and almost with the first puff, my self-possession began to assert itself. Whilst waiting for our drinks, we kept up a desultory conversation, but my eyes began to rove to obtain the information for which I was there. The room was an oblong one, of a fair size, at the top end was the bar, with rows of shelves nearly from floor to ceiling, backed with mirrors, and stocked with fancy bottles and glasses.

It was only the spread of sexually transmitted diseases that caused the army to reconsider. Officers were generally provided with condoms but ORs (other ranks) did without. In consequence, there were some 150,000 reported cases of venereal disease. Treatment involved a thirty-day stay in hospital and men were known to seek out infected prostitutes to gain the precious furlough away from the line:

Behind the rather high and well made counter, which stood before the shelves, were a couple of middle aged woman and a man. Down each side of the room ran a fixed seat with plush cushions. Just above the backs of the seats were a series of square mirrors, which reached almost to the ceiling, and were placed so closely together that only narrow strips of the wall could be seen between them. Along the bottom side, was also a long plush cushioned seat, but above its back were two window recesses, with a big square mirror between. The floor was of polished cement. The ceiling was picturesquely adorned with pictures, and plaster, big electric chandeliers hung from masses of fanciful plaster work.

Before the seats were placed many small tables, some of which had marble tops, and others of polished wood. The centre of the floor was quite clear. There were two doors that I could see, one was at the lower end, where we were sitting, but set in the side wall on our right. The other was a few paces from the counter, and set in the wall on our left. This, dear reader, is my best description of the room, I shall now start on the people in it, and a brief outline of their movements.

The room was pretty full, nearly all the tables were occupied. Here as on the street outside, a lot of the men were in the British uniforms. There were also Frenchmen of the French Army, and Navy and civilians. At the upper end of the seat, on the right hand wall, were two men busily dispensing music from a couple of melodeons.

At the tables were parties varying from two to half a dozen. Here and there a soldier or sailor or civilian, sat drinking and smoking, with a girl dressed in one flimsy garment and a wrap. At other tables were noisy groups of men with practically undressed girls on their knees, drinking and smoking, and laughing and singing. On the floor, half naked girls were dancing, with whoever would dance with them, while the waitresses all primly dressed in neat blouses and skirts, with white aprons, dodged about with orders for different tables.

Altogether the hubbub of talking and singing and laughing, the music and the swish, swishing of the dancers combined with the warm scented atmosphere made no wonder of the fact of my erstwhile bewilderment. Everything animate and inanimate seemed to breathe reckless, unheeding, shallow, mirth, and sensuous passion, and riotous licentious encouragement. The girls in the place I found ranged in ages from sixteen, to twenty four, and as I looked on their laughing painted faces, their very callousness sent a shiver of disgust through me.

All this I noticed in the space of a few moments, and while conversing with my chum. By the time the drinks arrived, I was talking fluently, and I was as self possessed as any man in the room. I had passed through my initiation to the happy hunting grounds of the libertines. As we sat sipping and talking, a young girl detached herself from among the dancers, and coming to our table, sat down and asked for a drink. I was surprised, not to say amused, at her coolness, but my pal evidently knew the ropes, and calling a passing waitress, he gave the required order as if he were treating his best friend. Me, being able to speak French fairly well, I assisted him in his conversation with her, and I also performed a similar service for her. These girls naturally get a smattering of English through frequent contact with English speaking people, but like all learners when in difficulty they revert to their mother tongue.

I had noticed, during my survey of the room that the door at the upper end was much in use, constantly men and women were passing through it and several times I had observed the same women, with different men. Now, I don't lay any claim to smartness as regards sagacity, but I certainly never considered myself slow at being able to put two and two together, I therefore summed up my thoughts on the meaning of the movements through that door, in one word, side-shows.

Whatever passed between that girl and my chum I can only guess, but they suddenly finished their glasses and rose. The only explanation I received from my pal at the time was a wink that might have meant a lot, and might have meant nothing. However, he followed her through the dancers towards the ever swinging door, and disappeared from my view. Left alone I ordered another drink, and lit a fresh cigarette. Before the drink arrived, I had a female companion; of course she wanted a drink too, so having learned this rope I ordered one for her.

Now I had come to this place as a cynic to learn about it without paying for my knowledge by risking my bodily health, consequently I had no desires to satisfy, beyond discretion.

Certainly as I looked into that woman's face, and saw what she was trying to hide by powder and paint, there was decidedly nothing to awaken any desires in me. In fact I actually felt my inner self recoiling. Nevertheless, I had fixed my face into a pleasant mask, because I was wanting something that she had and I had not – detailed information. I got a lot, but not all that I wanted, and being anxious to get to business, I was, even with drinks, unable to hold her longer. She was disappointed in not finding me in the mood for further intimacies, so she left for another table, as my chum and his lady friend returned.

The three of us sat drinking and smoking for a while, but as the lady seemed to desire to do me the favour she had already done my chum, I said to myself, 'not yet my son' and stated that it was time to be making for camp. Our heads were a bit light when we got out of that place that night, but we had had a good time in our different ways, and we both thought we had received value for our money.

It was some little time later, that I obtained all the enlightenment I required, and I was wise enough to use it to my own personal benefit, when occasions occurred. Needless to say I also had to pass through the ever swinging door to complete my education, and to be able to speak from personal experience. In justice to myself though, I did not become a victim of libertinism.

Meanwhile, those other realities of war were waiting.

Notes

1. John Buchan, *The History of the Royal Scots Fusiliers 1678–1918*, Naval & Military Press Ltd (2005).

3

THE SOLDIER

Arthur was on his way to being 'blooded'. That vast cauldron, the Western Front, was sucking in more and more victims. As the war progressed its scale intensified rather than diminished. The armies of 1917–18 would be enormous compared to those who had marched (seemingly so joyful) to war in 1914:

> Monday 21 May 1917: I rose fine and fit this morning and prepared for breakfast of bully beef and dog biscuits and tea, after which the dreaded march was to commence. The draft started about 8 a.m. and after a gruelling march [of 29km], the thought of which I shall never forget, it arrived in Étaples about 3.45 p.m. in a nearly exhausted condition, for the weather was terribly hot. After a good night's rest the remainder of our training will be resumed.

Étaples; the 'Bull Ring': this unassuming fishing village some 24km south of Boulogne had, by 1917, become notorious as a version of 'boot camp' – the major British training area for those embarking for the Calvary of the Western Front:

Tuesday 22 May 1917: Our draft has had a fine easy day today but tomorrow we expect to go to the 'Bull Ring', a place where the soldier gets put through the mill in style before going up to the trenches. The weather has been fearfully hot and I am drinking like a whale.

Wednesday 23 May 1917: Our crowd was at the 'Bull Ring' today and what a day. No wonder they call it the 'Bull Ring'. It is only three miles from camp but I never had such a tramp in my life. The sun blazed and there was hardly a breeze. We were through all kinds of gases and what with nearly suffocating us, gassing us and then marching us back again with the blazing sun making our steel helmets like red hot pudding basins we were just about dead on arriving about 5 p.m. being away since 8 a.m. Oh what a day!

The Bull Ring was justifiably notorious: endless drill and bayonet practice, gruelling forced marches over the spongy carpet of the dunes in full kit, sweat building in the woollen furnace of thick khaki. Instructors, both officers and NCOs, were branded 'canaries' – most were said never to have been anywhere near the front line:

Thursday 24 May 1917: No 'Bull Ring' today. Thank God. We were paraded at 9.30 a.m. for baths which we all badly needed. At 12 a.m. we paraded again to wash our shirts etc. Mine needed scrubbing badly. This morning I saw about fourteen hundred Anzacs embarking in cattle trucks for the line. They seemed quite cheery as the band stood playing while they were passing from the platform. This sight cheered me up considerably. The rest of the day passed uneventfully.

Friday 25 May 1917: This morning at 6.45 a.m. we started for the dreaded 'Bull Ring'. On reaching there we were instructed in the art of trench warfare. My first duty was to guard the latrine. But as we were the first arrivals no one had used it so I had no gas to contend with. On reaching camp the weekly supply of fags were dished out. Our section goes on Zeppelin piquet tonight but I don't think anything will happen. However it remains to be seen. One never knows, does one!

Saturday 26 May 1917: There were no Zepps [Zeppelins] last night so we slept in peace. We were at the 'Range' this morning until dinner time. In the afternoon we marched to the 'Bull Ring'. We put up some new dummies and returned about 6.30 p.m. There is no Saturday half-day out here and it's doubtful if we get tomorrow to ourselves. The weather is fearfully hot but I can stick it fine.

Zeppelins, named after their inventor, Count von Zeppelin, were a nineteenth-century design for a rigid airship and first flew in 1910. The Germans employed them as bombers throughout the war, though by 1917 they were becoming obsolete and being replaced by four-engine aircraft. They were still dreaded, a vast cigar-shaped talisman of terror, floating serenely and, at that time, above fighter ceiling, their glittering silvered hulls disgorging death from the skies. Both troops and civilians would, for the first time, experience the terrors of aerial bombing:

Sunday 27 May 1917: We got today off all-right. I drew my pay (5 francs) got my meals and stewed in the heat. I went to the pictures this evening. A novel experience for a Sunday evening, but then a soldier's life is full of novel experiences if it comes to that.

Monday 28 May 1917: We were at the 'Bull Ring' again today. The draft is expecting to go up the line some time this week so I'm looking forward to the departing day.

It was said that wounded men, ostensibly recuperating at Étaples, found the regime so oppressive, they preferred to return to the trenches. Wilfred Owen memorably described the 'look' of the men there, not the savage or fearful face of battle, yet not an expression that would ever be seen in Civvy Street. It was a form of blank intensity, almost inhuman:

Tuesday 29 May 1917: 'Bull Ring' as usual today. Walking in this scorching heat with full (90 lb) pack is something awful. This evening my very braces were soaking with sweat. I received my Balmoral this evening and other things to complete my trench kit.

Wednesday 30 May 1917: The 'Bull Ring' was our lot today again. This place is nothing but sand dunes. It is nice to lie on but rotten to walk on, but however I'm getting used to sand-dancing now.

Long after Arthur's time at the Bull Ring, on 9 September 1917, simmering frustration and friction flared into discontent and finally mutiny amongst non-commissioned men passing through the base camp at Étaples. The military police panicked and opened fire, killing one Tommy and injuring a French civilian. They were chased clear of the base and order was only restored days later. One of the alleged mutineers from the Royal Northumberland Fusiliers was shot and others gaoled. It was altogether a shameful incident, not the BEF's finest hour:

Thursday 31 May 1917: 'Bull Ring' again. Nothing fresh, I'm getting used to the sand dancing (now).

Friday 1 June 1917: We again went to the 'Bull Ring' today. I thought the first day was bad but today was worse. The heat was something terrific. When we had covered a mile or more a fellow dropped in a fit through the heat. Throughout the whole day fellows were fainting for want of water. The water has been cut off for three days so that there was none even to wash ourselves with. While returning a motor ran over a fellow's leg. This has been a day of accidents. Fags were dished out today.

Saturday 2 June 1917: The 'Ring' was sprung on us again today but we got it easy for a wonder. We are supposed to be finished with the 'Ring' now but we might have to go back again tomorrow. As it's pay-day tomorrow we are kind of cheery. Sunday in the army only lasts until after church so I can visit the pictures tomorrow.

Sunday 3 June 1917: The first thing we had this morning was kit inspection. Pay was next after C.O.'s inspection. The draft was put under orders for the front this afternoon. Some of us were transferred to the R.S.F. [Royal Scots Fusiliers]. As I write this the rations are being divided out, midst yells, shouts and other indescribable sounds, preparatory to departing tomorrow. There will be ructions among the boys as it's the last night here.

Chemin de fer – courtesy of French Railways: one of the Tommies' enduring memories of France was of the French railway system. While officers might travel in compartments, men and horses shared identical transport arrangements – cattle trucks. These were cramped, insanitary and, above all, unimaginably slow. The vast, lumbering troop trains chugged and jolted, often at less than an arthritic walking pace, across Northern France. For the time taken this might have been as wide as a prairie or as deep as the steppe. Flat land, uninteresting, small towns and villages with unpronounceable, forgettable names blended with unending discomfort and tedium. Frequently the trains simply stopped, and stayed stopped, for ages for no apparent reason; then, equally mysteriously, would clank heavily forward. Arthur's experience was to prove no exception:

> Monday 4 June 1917: This morning we marched to our special train of horse boxes. The train started about 8.15 a.m. on its slow lumbering journey. The comic events which took place during the journey are too numerous to mention but I laughed myself sore. Arguments were varied and plentiful, but on coming within sound of the guns the arguments ceased and opinions ran in unison. The rest camp was reached about 11.45 p.m. but we were so interested in the flashes and noise of distant artillery that for a time we forgot bed. However drowsiness soon asserted itself and we remembered.

Truly a soldier's life is a tangled skein of ways and means to curious ends, but more anon, so gentle reader, read on. Ask any Expeditionary Force man for his opinion of the French railways, and you'll likely hear words that you never dreamed existed in the English language. Strictly speaking in all probability they do not. If you are any good at deducing, you'll be able to guess what the poor chap is trying to convey to you.

As I am, or rather have been, an Expeditionary Force man, if you wish to retain a respectable opinion of me, please don't ask for my version on French railways. Should you like to know the reason for our (ex-Tommies) strong or critical opinion, then on behalf and in defence of our unanimous verdict, I'll proceed to enlighten you. Before I start it must be remembered that the sections of railways I speak of ran into and about the war zone. By this statement I am at least, giving the railways a chance of any leniency of judgment, which you ... might be pleased to pass on to them.

For his grand war-winning offensive Haig was hamstrung by political doubters. The War Cabinet was insisting on adequate French support for his main attack. In the circumstances, this appeared highly improbable. It was not until 25 July that he was given the green light. The intervening weeks had given Rupprecht the breathing space he needed and Flanders weather was clearly with him. Flanders ('Flooded Land') was low-lying and clay based.

Generations of patient farmers had corralled the waters by ingenious irrigation and drainage, but three years of neglect and endless churning of shells had destroyed their clever systems. The summer of 1917 was exceptionally wet. Mud was the prevailing characteristic of Flanders that year. A mud so omnipresent, so cloying, so lethal, waiting to suck the heavily laden down into its black heart, that it has come to define our memory of the forthcoming battle.

The Allied plan called for a saturation bombardment of the German Flanders position. At 15 miles in length the attack front-age was a large one, but the key objectives lay within the shorter span between Boesinghe and the Zillebeke-Zandvoorde Road, a distance of some 7½ miles. To the north, Gough's Fifth Army would commit four full corps. Plumer's Second Army would undertake a strictly subsidiary assault to the south. As an element in this, the RSF would attack as part of 15th and 30th Divisions' assault with three battalions up, 2nd (Arthur), 6th and 7th:

Tuesday 5 June 1917: We had a fine easy day today; nothing to do except one or two inspections and to listen to the guns and watch aeroplanes and observation balloons. Tomorrow we carry on as per usual.

War is rarely exciting. The grand, Homeric clash of arms occurs but rarely. Most is tedium, routine, bull and boredom. Readers who expect war diaries to be full of violent action or observations on grand strategy are apt to be disappointed. Arthur's diary, keenly observed as it is, remains the diary of the ordinary soldier, 'Tommy Atkins':

Wednesday 6 June 1917: The day was fairly easy owing to the great heat. Tomorrow we are to join our regiment and the brigade [90th Brigade of 30th Division, Second Army]. The air is full of sounds of whizzing shells, booming guns and popping of aircraft guns.

Thursday 7 June 1917: This has been a good day for the allies. Hill 60 was blown up early this morning [Messines Ridge]. Later several batches of prisoners were brought in. We joined our battalion about 4.45 p.m. The fellows seem a decent lot. There was a thunder storm this afternoon. There being no room I had to sleep under a cart which I did with ease.

Friday 8 June 1917: It has been a very easy day. I attended a small service this afternoon before going into the line. At this moment of writing I am waiting word to start our journey on foot which will be a night affair as far as I can see. I sent home my first letter today.

Saturday 9 June 1917: I am now writing this in a dugout in the second line trenches. We arrived here very early this morning after a short walk, a short train journey and a very long march, dodging shell holes, tree stumps etc. all the way. We are expecting to go into the front line tonight [Ypres].

Winters in Flanders are inhospitable, cold, wet with a dank wind that whips in over the North Sea. Mud freezes; keeping out the insidious cold becomes a priority. Summers tend to be muggy and often wet. Where ground permitted, trenches would be dug down some 8ft, and would be about 12ft wide. A shelf or firestep was built into the forward-facing flank to form a fighting platform. Sandbags were used to form a parapet and, to the rear, a parados. The former was generally lower than the latter so defenders' profiles would be broken up and thus less exposed to snipers. Distances between the opposing lines could be half a mile or only a matter of yards. Trench sides, even in firm, dry chalk upland, would not stand without support. Timber and corrugated iron had to be brought in and fatigue parties kept busy, hour after exhausting hour, maintaining the structure.

A trench was never a purely linear feature. If it were, once penetrated by the enemy, gaining a foothold could rake the entire length. Instead, they were built as an alternating system of projecting fire-bays and traverses (those sections that provided linkage). To attack such a trench involved 'bombing up the traverses'. An attacking section would be divided between 'bombers' (those who threw grenades) and 'bayonet' men. The former lobbed their bombs over the fire-bay and the latter rushed the traverse ready to deal with any surviving enemy who might have fight left in them – a dreadful attritional slogging match. Snipers were a constant and deadly menace.

No battalion spent the whole of its time actually in the trenches themselves. Service in the line was followed by a period in reserve, punctuated by welcome – if usually all too brief – spells of relative repose, though poor billets often merited more censure than an ill-sited or badly finished trench:

I first actually entered the trenches on the dawn of the 9th June 1917, I can tell you, after our grueling march decribed in the diary, I was a physical wreck. That night as I plumped down in a dugout, I was so tired that without taking off my equipment, I almost immediately fell into a trance. All the Kaiser's horses and all the Kaiser's men, could not have put the wind up me that night. No, I was too far beyond the stage of self preservation. Sleep and welcome oblivion was wanted. I believe I should not have cared, if I had been told I should never wake again. I craved rest in sleep, and I simply slept. How long I remained in the tender arms of Morpheus I know not, but it was darkening towards another evening when I awoke, very stiff but with a greater interest in things in general. I soon learned that we were to proceed to the front line in a few hours.

After dark, the word was passed down the trench to harness up and be ready to move. I was feeling very mucky with the dirt, and dried sweat of the previous night, clogging my skin. I was only a rookie then, but later these inconveniences were taken as a matter of course. All being ready, we set off in single file, up the trench with warnings coming down the file of 'broken duckboards, shaky duckboards, slanting duckboards, missing duckboards' and to tell the truth, I never thought that duckboards had so many deficiencies, and I might say tricks. I dare-say you'll laugh at the idea of the performing duck-boards, but I know to my cost, some of them are jolly fine acrobats. I might write of some of their stunts some day, if I have time and space.

On we went round corners, and corners, and still more corners, while the very lights gave us glimpses now and then of our very confined surroundings. The pace was just an ordinary walking pace, so we had time to pick our way when necessary. An occasional splash or clatter, finished neatly off by a display of extraordinary and prolonged elocution showed that the duckboards were waiting for the unwary. My pal at this time was walking in front of me, and he led me that night without my once coming to grief. Later I was to miss his valued instruction and become one of the many, many victims of the acrobatic duckboards.

Through time we entered the front line, and in the placing of the various platoons, our platoon was on the extreme right of the half battalion, the other half battalion was in supports. I was told off for first watch, and I must say my first look across no man's land was very disappointing to me. I expected to see corpses lying here, and these with an occasional gun lying on its side, and perhaps a horse or two. Ah! Said I, when I had looked in vain for the horrors of war, 'war is not what it's cracked up to be, I see now how much these artists exaggerate'. All I saw was a barren stretch of well churned earth, disappearing into the gloom, and sparsely dotted with distorted remains of the tree trunks.

Suddenly a couple of Verey lights shot into the air, coming down in a big green blaze. Within the radius of the blaze I discerned running across my front, many tangled lengths of barbed wire. This wire was about twenty yards out. I was greatly amused with the fireworks, and I think the relieving chaps saw this, and I was left to enjoy the spectacle all night. I don't know what I should have done if the Jerrys had come over, because I was not even, thinking of them.

I remember thinking after I had been posted, that more explicit orders might have been given me, as I was only a new hand. When the corporal informed me that I was to take first watch I said 'What have I to do?' he said 'This your first time?' I only guessed what he meant, but I said 'Yes.' 'Well,' said he, 'just stand up on that step and shoot anybody you see who looks like a German.' He was walking away when turning suddenly he said, 'By the by, have you ever seen a German?' I told him that I had come in contact with German barbers and waiters. 'Ahem,' muttered the corporal becoming vastly amused, 'if you see anybody call the other chaps at once, we've got a patrol out and they won't like being mistaken for Germans.'

Then as a parting shot, as he went off up the trench he said, 'Be sure and don't hesitate to tell the others because if it happens to be Jerrys there may be one or two good barbers amongst 'em.' These were my instructions, but as I have said the novelty of the fireworks sent all orders from my head in a very short time. Happily nothing happened that night, and I really wondered what the people at home were making such a fuss about. This was only another case of 'Where ignorance is Bliss'.

The night wore on, but the interest in the Verey lights maintained its power over me, thus I sleepily saw the dawn brightening towards another day, and the Verey lights losing their emerald brilliance. With daylight came the order to stand down – there is no parapet watch kept during the day unless by periscope.

The Bosche was very quiet, and the sun coming out, the morning mists thinned away, and the day became milder; so I cooped myself up in an old box that was upended beside the fire-step, and fell asleep. Tea was dished out about five o'clock, so I was wakened up to part take [*sic*] of the refreshing beverage. It does not take a man on active service long to dispose of his allowance of rations, so you may conclude that in a very short time I had resumed my sleeping post.

After a couple of hours or so, I took the notion to have a look round, and it was during this limited ramble that I discovered several small wooden crosses at the back of the trench. Now as a rule graves have sobering effects upon most people, according to their temperament, all I can say is, that those graves set me thinking, and I saw that here was one cause of the fuss made by the people at home. Later in the day, our platoon officer came giving instructions, and making arrangements for a raid which we were to make on the enemy trenches that night. The effect of the raid was to get prisoners and information.

Speaking for myself I was delighted, and I wondered why the other chaps looked so serious. Why here was I expecting to see men hacking and stabbing and shooting in truth to tell, my own boyish imagination was so vivid, that in my inmost self I was afraid; but instead what did I find, a nice bright day, fellows lying about smoking, reading or yarning. Nothing whatever to disturb the calm serenity, but an occasional solemn boom of an odd gun now and then, the sound if anything harmonised with our lackadaisical inclinations. Can it be expected, that after this pleasant self delusion, I should even vaguely realise what a raid on the enemy trenches would be like?

Gradually as the day drew to a close, the German artillery fire increased, and by dark the stutter of machine-guns had become more voluble. Up to now I had seen nothing but the Verey lights to excite my curiosity, and the significance of this exchanging of ammunition, held no warning for me. Eagerly I waited for the start of the expedition into no man's land, so judge of my disappointment, and my comrades' relief, when the officer came with the news that the raid was off. That night we were manning the parapet with gas helmets on, and everything ready to give Jerry a warm reception. While the shells were whizzing and bursting overhead, I was much amused, with the other chaps bobbing up and down, and jumping into corners at every near burst. I must say at that moment I felt much superior as I stood on the fire-step without a movement.

This is no boast dear reader, for you must understand, that in my ignorance, guns and shells were only but sounds to me and I had never seen the effects of shell-fire. Jerry eased off about dawn, and things were fairly peaceful until about six o'clock, then he showed us the results of his gun practice, and I can tell you when Jerry lets himself go in those days he was generosity personified in handing out his shells.

Still I lounged nonchalantly about the trench, for had not the drill instructors at home told us that sounds would do us no harm and were nothing to be afraid of. About twelve o'clock, the bombardment almost died out, and the boys looked as if a great weight had been removed from their minds. The night was a similar but quieter edition of the previous one, and in fact the following two days and nights were identical in their routine and events.

Exactly at 6 a.m. the bombardment would commence in earnest, and continue in a perfect fury until twelve noon; then dying away all would be peaceful until dark, when a desultory fire would last until dawn, a relapse again taking place until 6 a.m. when the fire would be repeated. The 14th June 1917 dawned with the usual chilly mist, but knowing we should have peace until a few hours hence, after wrapping ourselves in our great coats we lay down, if not to sleep, to ease our feet.

Boom! Bang! Whiz! Crunch! Six o'clock, by gum we were getting it hard this morning. Jerry's got our range at last so it's heaven help us. Nothing tries the nerves so much, as to have to sit still under a bombardment. So far I was not so affected as I otherwise might have been if I had known more about shell-fire; but fear is infectious, and I began to think that after all there must be something in the grim way the men around me went about. The six hours passed eventually without any damage being done in our vicinity. Now during our one day in supports, and up to this our fourth day in the front line, we had had no opportunity of washing ourselves, so you may guess we were greater strangers to soap than we cared to admit. At the same time our substitute for linen was occupied by a seemingly prosperous population.

The day by this time was fine and warm so with my friend on my arm, I made my way down our poor old battered trench until I came to a deserted part. Here I laid down my bundock, took off my equipment and tunic and shirt, and sitting down drew my grey back across my knees, and the slaughter commenced. For about an hour and a half I slew, and slew [lice were a constant affliction], yea I slew exceedingly. None found was spared, and my thumb-nails fully testified the fact. Desisting at last however, I made preparations for returning to my own part of the trench. I was soon ready and with the air of one who has performed an unpleasant operation to his entire satisfaction, I sauntered along the way I had come.

What a lovely day it was, and how quiet everything was. As I meandered along watching the H.E. [high explosive] bursting like masses of cotton wool high up in the sky, my thoughts were as far away from my surroundings then, as those little lumps of cotton wool. On I moved, mechanically following the twists and turns of the trench, and turning a corner, my absent minded gaze alighted on.

Oh Heavens! What an awful sight. Five years have elapsed from that time of writing this, but that first dead soldier is a sight that is practically photographed on my brain. At that sight, it was as if my ruminations had been cast from their exalted altitude of self contentedness, to an abyss of nauseating realities.

In the first instant I saw every detail, yet the very horribleness of the sight kept my eyes riveted longer on the gruesome thing. The shell had burst right in the middle of the trench, so that now for several yards there was no trench. On the sloping side of the crater lay somebody's son. To me the poor corpse lay like a rag doll with all the stuffing out of it, and just flung down as if in anger or haste. The uniform was almost one big brownish red stain. The equipment appeared as if some bigger man had just hung it on the body, it was a mass of tangled straps and buckles. The reason was only too apparent. The whole of the victim's back had been almost blown out. Death in many cases shows itself in the unnatural position of the dead.

Death in this case seemed to have used its most grotesque inspirations on this poor lad. The head lay near the edge of the crater and half buried in the loose earth, one arm was also buried in the earth, the body lay partly on its side, and the other arm dropped over the back. From the hips the body might have belonged to another man altogether, the legs in fact defied all laws pertaining to the structure of the human frame.

My first sight of an offering to Thor. Was my imagination, proof against the feeling that arose within me? No! decidedly No! I had imagined dead men it is true, but only like those seen in the cinematograph, no blood, no distortion of the face and limbs, but lying as if they were comfortably sleeping. In those few moments, my blood froze in my veins; the awful thing fascinated yet revulsed [*sic*] me. The shock and the grip of inaction passed however, and instead of passing on, I turned and blindly staggered round a friendly corner. I would not, at that time, have passed the gruesome thing for anything. As I went vaguely back, my senses seemed benumbed and though the day was just as grand yet it seemed vastly changed some-how, but for what reason I cannot say.

I soon reached my former seat, and flopping helplessly down, I made strenuous efforts to regain my self control. I succeeded at length, and with a great self show of determination, I set off again fully decided that this time I should reach my position supposing there were dead men all the way. As I came near the fatal spot, which I seemed to do very quickly in spite of my slow pace, I inwardly tightened up my self control and quickened my pace. Before I turned the dreaded corner, I kept my head reverted from one side of the shell crater. The churned up soil would not allow of my quickening speed, but with my steel helmet waggling all over my head I stumbled over the loose earth and it was a relief to step into the continuation of the trench.

Much as a sight may cause the revulsion of feelings, some people get a sudden craving at the time to have just a last momentary glance. This feeling came over me so with a clear trench before me, I cast a sudden look over my shoulder. There was the crater right enough, and a strap or two lying on the side, but the corpse was gone, completely vanished.

Judge of my surprise and the tinge of shame that came over me, when I thought of how I had passed that shell hole if not in panic then most certain in haste; the thing had been removed, while I had been pulling myself together further down the trench. Truly the people at home had a great deal to make a fuss of when their dear men came back. Yes, I saw it all now, I realised it all now and I appreciated it all now. Fate however takes no half measures and it intended that I should see, realise, and appreciate, even more but it had at least put my nerve and control through the first process of strengthening.

That night, we were relieved and as the diary states we received a warm, if not pleasant reception in passing 'Hell Fire Corner'. That was really my baptism of fire, and incidentally where I also learned the habit of ducking!

Death in battle was not the only hazard Tommies faced. Major actions were relatively rare but random shelling, sniping and sheer bad luck ensured a steady flow of casualties whenever the battalion was 'up'. An indispensable feature of the trench-fighter's troglodyte existence was the dugout. Generally, this limited accommodation was reserved for officers, while ORs had to scrape shelters or 'funk-holes' in the sides of the trench:

Sunday 10 June 1917: We reached the front line about midnight. I am going on patrol tonight. Things are very quiet.

Monday 11 June 1917: Business got very busy last night so the patrol party didn't go out. Jerry is bombarding us pretty heavily. A gas attack is expected. Things cooled down again until Jerry sent over some more gas shells. The Boche has our trenches marked off anyway.

Tuesday 12 June 1917: Jerry is still noticing us and paying us compliments.

Wednesday 13 June 1917: Still Jerry is banging away good-o. He's giving us an example of how his artillery does it.

Patrolling was a particular feature of trench warfare. British tactical doctrine emphasised the need to take the fight to the enemy, to maintain our morale and diminish his by taking control of no man's land. Any attempt to roam over the blasted heath between the two armies was certain death by day and hazardous in the extreme by night. Patrols might involve a handful of men led by an NCO seeking intelligence and prisoners or a full battalion-sized raid aimed at seriously 'biffing' the foe and wresting either tactical gains or seriously buffeting enemy morale:

Thursday 14 June 1917: Jerry has nearly demolished our trenches. He is like clock work. He starts regularly at 12 a.m. and finishes at 6 p.m. We are shifting out tonight so I can get what I haven't had for five days, a wash and a good sleep.

Increasingly, artillery was becoming queen of the battlefield, the dominant arm. The earlier shell scandals of 1915 and failures on the Somme had been bitter lessons but both sides were steadily improving, the gunners more technically proficient:

Friday 15 June 1917: We cleared out between 12 p.m. and 1 p.m. last night. On the way we had to pass through the transport. Just as we reached it, Jerry started shelling at the rate of about 10 to 15 shells a minute. As this was the only way out we had to move at the double and scattering all ways it was every man for himself. The night was very dark and we were stumbling into shell holes, shattered huts, wrecked wagons, dead mules, fallen trees, barbed wire, broken harness wagon chains, discarded packs and rifles, petrol tins and suchlike. I suppose Jerry had caught the transport unexpectedly thus causing confusion and complete wreckage.

It was one of the ironies of industrial age warfare that most transport was still horse-drawn, a function that hadn't changed in centuries. This business of logistical support was mundane and unglamorous; it was also very dangerous work:

The night was terribly hot. We were blinded with sweat but we had to keep moving at the double and dodging what was left of the ill-fated transport which was galloping from the spot. The mules were half mad with fear, the drivers excited. The motors were tearing along as if they had a clear road and heedless of running down the nearly exhausted infantry. This was my baptism of fire. I heard after that this was called 'Shrapnel Corner' or 'Hell's Fire Corner'. I never saw a place so well named before or since. I slept well on reaching camp never-the-less. I saw two runners buried today. This is the first burial on active service I have seen.

Saturday 16 June 1917: Things are going as well as can be expected today. I saw an observation balloon catch fire through heat. I don't know whether the observers escaped. In the evening we were carrying gas shells under fire. It was awful as the shells were very heavy. [Dickebushe]

Sunday 17 June 1917: I spent a lazy day and I received a letter of bad news from home.

Monday 18 June 1917: Today passed quietly. We are expected to shift to another camp a mile away. I wrote several letters home.

Tuesday 19 June 1917: The shift was made about 12 p.m. last night. This morning I awoke to find the rain simply pouring. As I was sleeping in the open it was very unpleasant. This is the first rain I've seen since landing.

Letters home were the Tommy's balm, his link with that other reality, the one he'd left so very far behind. It was a subaltern's duty to censor the men's correspondence, a duty many found distasteful but no hint which might aid the enemy was allowed:

Wednesday 20 June 1917: Another quiet day, the weather is still wet but very hot; shifting tonight.

Thursday 21 June 1917: This morning we took the road. A train helped us a lot of the way.

Friday 22 June 1917: We are now out of sound of the guns and the country looks like it should look. Not devastated and blood-soaked.

Saturday 23 June 1917: This place is so glorious. I could stay here forever. We had inspection and fags were issued this afternoon. The question is will we be paid this week?

Like most of his comrades, Arthur was not overly preoccupied by thoughts of king and country. Such sentiments, where they were present at the outset, soon vanished, it was far more important to be paid on time:

> Sunday 24 June 1917: The day passed quietly. No pay yet.

> Monday 25 June 1917: The routine of parading started today. I received a letter from one of the girls saying a parcel and box was coming. No pay yet.

> Tuesday 26 June 1917: We are still awaiting pay. The battalion starts for the trenches tomorrow.

> Wednesday 27 June 1917: The half-way billet has been reached and we are happy. The pay has come at last. Hurrah!

Reality was about endless fatigues, discomfort and the omnipresent risk of sudden and impersonal death from random shell or mortar:

> Thursday 28 June 1917: Our destination was reached this morning. I spent my last 4d. Roll on Pay-day. [Dickebusche]

> Friday 29 June 1917: The working party was off last night thank God. This is really cushy.

> Saturday 30 June 1917: We never went to work last night so much the better. Nothing doing here at all. This is a very cushy time for us.

> Sunday 1 July 1917: There was a voluntary church service but as there was no C of E service I didn't go. We are going to work tonight. Jerry has dropped a few shells near us but did no harm except blew up a dump.

Monday 2 July 1917: Last night the work was the quietest job I've been on. There was one narrow shave a shell dropped within ten yards of the party but thank God it was a dud. I received a letter and parcel today it was like a gift from heaven.

Tuesday 3 July 1917: Jerry is now paying us his best attention. He shelled us out of our camp this morning. In our new position we are safe till Jerry finds us again.

Wednesday 4 July 1917: Jerry's found us. He started by shelling the stables killing one man wounded six, killing seven horses and wounding several others.

Thursday 5 July 1917: Things are quiet today. We are expecting to shift back tomorrow.

Friday 6 July 1917: We started at 5.30 a.m. this morning and with the magnificent train service we did an hour's journey in four and a half hours. As we are only half way we resume the march tomorrow. The weather is glorious now.

Not being intimate with the brass-hats, of course, we're only privates, we have no idea of our destination, but we conclude it must be a fairish distance away, seeing we have a train to convey us. In the early morning, soon after breakfast, we 'fall in' and march away to the rail-head, where our train awaits us. Gentle reader; allow me to digress a little to put a curious fact before you.

If you went to catch a train at one of your local stations, and on entering the platform, you saw passenger coaches on the side, and cattle trucks on the other side of it, you would without the least thought enter a coach. If a cow also entered the platform would it consider which conveyance to enter? I wonder! Perhaps you'll get an idea from the next illustration.

The Tommy in France is taken to catch the train. There are two trains in, a coach train, and a truck train. Instinctively, Tommy gazes on the trucks, invariably marked 'Hommes 40 Cheveaux 8', in English, meaning 40 men 8 horses, the carriages are for his superiors.

Perhaps the insinuation is rather marked, but if the rank and file received the cattle's portion then the fact is obvious. Well reader, we'll resume the experience. We are ordered to mount the cattle trucks, and for a space, we busy ourselves preparing a spot in the truck we select.

Having dumped our equipment and rifles on our claim, we descend and go on the scrounge. Soldiers always use their spare time in scrounging. The trains usually start about an hour after the troops have boarded them, so if an *estaminet* is handy (it always is) we can drop in and pass the time. When we reach the café, we find we are by no means the first to be inspired with such a good way of spending a weary hour. By and by the whistle blows, but unhurriedly we finish our drinks, and whilst the newer hands scramble and rush past us, we stroll leisurely out, and with a few dignified quick steps, we board the train as our truck reaches us. There is an art in boarding a moving vehicle, no matter how slow it moves, with dignity, watched by criticising eyes. Try boarding a car with a few friends watching, and you'll find your dignity well tested.

It is a strange thing, but I've often noticed that all the hard cases find themselves in the same trucks. Let us suppose (just for him of course) that we are hard cases. 'Any money?' somebody cries. The gamblers answer, 'Where's the cards?' A greasy well thumbed pack is produced and a ring is formed in the centre of the truck. Not being over flush ourselves (it doesn't do to suppose too much), we keep what we've got for the future, and better application. Real hard cases are cute! Watch us.

The day being fine, we'll crush ourselves in the door-way of the truck, and sit with our legs dangling outside over the floor. The train is now moving about ten miles an hour, it keeps at this rate for some time, until we are beginning to mistake it for an express. Suddenly it jolts to a standstill, and with a sigh, the mistaken identity of the train to an express is acknowledged. The most of the boys who are not gambling, jump down, and take a walk along the track, or go foraging about any trucks that may happen to be on the siding. Twenty minutes may pass, but at last the whistle goes, and off we stumble again.

We, having walked ahead, simply wait for the train to reach us. Eight miles an hour is about the pace at this time and things are becoming monotonous. Soon we are rumbling past a siding of trucks but eagle eyes have spotted apples in those trucks and from the nearer side of our train, there pours forth from every truck, streams of eager fruit-loving Tommies (gamblers included).

The train rumbles on, but the apple raid goes merrily if hastily on, and quite a generous supply is carried to the raiders trucks. You may depend that the most is made of the opportunity, for it is not every day we get our fill of apples for the taking. Those apple trucks are considerably less full after our train of fighting lads has passed, than they were before we arrived.

Anyhow, as we say, if the Frenchmen want us to help them keep the Germans out of France, they shouldn't grudge us a few apples. They do though, and the C.O. will jolly soon receive a complaint, and we will in turn receive a lecture, but bless my soul, we consider all fruit trucks as lawful loot, so the lectures are swallowed; but so are the contents of the fruit-trucks which we happen across.

For a space of a few hours everybody is interested in apples, and stumps are left scattered profusely in the track of the train.

On and on trundles the horse-boxes, and like Alexander, we long for fresh fields to conquer, or rather I should say, fresh trucks to raid. Suddenly a very old timer informs us, that we are nearing a coal dump. Good News! We are getting chilly.

The word is passed along, and preparations for the coal raid are at once commenced. All the empty petrol tins and buckets, etc. (the results of our scrounging expeditions) are brought to light. Soon the chaps of the forward trucks are seen slipping over the rails with bags, and buckets and we take the tip and do likewise. No time is lost in securing the black diamonds and the raid is carried through with a rapidity and coolness (sheer cheek if you like) that shows we are raiders of no small merits. Before we are a half mile further on, smoke is issuing from nearly every truck, and the boys are looking to their water bottles for water to drum up. Just at this moment the train again shuffles to a halt.

Sighting some dwellings about a quarter of a mile further on, we find our smoke-dried throats are bothering us, or perhaps it is the apples, but anyway the only remedy lies somewhere near those dwellings. Immediately we start forward and true to our intuition, we see an *estaminet* on our arrival. Of the three quarters of an hour that the train stands, we spend about forty minutes at our retreat. We board our truck as it comes abreast of us and taking our usual seat we admire the scenery, while we jog along at what I think was the maximum ten miles an hour. Whatever monarch said 'My Kingdom for a Horse' must have travelled, I'm sure, on one of these trains.

It is now shortly after mid-day, and once again the train ceases it's perambulation of the track. We have always an open eye for a soldier's rest (an *estaminet*), so again we go in search of a place to dispose of some of our worldly wealth. Observe the wisdom of restraint from gambling. As we surreptitiously pass the engine, dodging the officers, the driver and his mate, are opening their dinners, and unscrewing their wine bottles.

The revolution has certainly left behind a national determination in the minds of the working class, not to be driven, or deprived of natural requirements if possible. Consequently the French workman keeps strictly within the regular working period, and he has made the promptitude of knocking off an art.

We know that at least about half an hour will be required for the engineer's meal, so the sooner we are ensconced in some fair retreat; the longer will be our enjoyment of it. Forward has for long been a soldier's motto, so forward we go, because it is easier and looks better, to wait for a train, than to run after it. As I have inferred before, we are seldom wrong in surmising the proximity of a soldier's rest and as this case is no exception, in a very short time we are lying back, whilst our wants are being attended to.

It is said, that women are great posers, that is very likely, but suppose they posed for a life time, I don't think they could extract the same gratification from doing so, that the Tommy on foreign service can gentle reader, it really produces an exquisite sensation, to saunter into a café, with a nonchalant air, and our heavy boots ringing on the flag-stones (in a country café), with our decided manly military tread.

Still more exquisite is it, to lower oneself into an easy seat, like a veritable Hercules, after his labours and drink wine like Ulysses, testing his well earned sack while the hostess and serving girl send sly glances in our direction. Perhaps the kiddies, whilst they regard us in round-eyed wonder, are a bit disappointed, because we have no guns or swords with us, but we sometimes feel for their sakes, that we could trail them about with us. (The guns and swords, mind not the kids.)

Like true heroes, we pretend to take no notice of our admirers, and with sage nods, and languid gesticulations, we converse in a monotone, common to people who are cognisant of the fact of their popularity, and wish by a favourable impression, to support it. In spite of our seeming indifference of things around us, our ears are open to catch the sound of the whistle, and at last we hear it.

With a sigh, we heave ourselves to our feet, and setting our shoulders, we give our (in this case) buxom hostess a gallant farewell, and with a brisk, but well controlled walk, we make for the metals. We find the gamblers still engrossed in their get rich quick idea, but the number is sadly reduced. The fire is going well and also roasted apples. The engineers' wives must have dished out good dinners today, because the old 'Puffing Billy' is jostling along at nearly twelve miles an hour, as near as can be judged.

I have noticed that the troops are never happier, than when going anywhere at a decent speed. Snatches of songs are reaching us on the breeze, and we also are affected with a desire for vocal efforts. Now, when Tommy sings, he sings with a will, but he is not the least sensitive as regards the subject selected; but then no pleasure is derived, unless the songs are suitable to the company.

The afternoon is wearing on now, still no solution to the mystery of our destination has been found. Suddenly the train slows to nearly a walking pace, and continues so for a considerable distance. The lights of well scattered dwellings are faintly twinkling through the dusk, and with the reddening of the sky, the wind takes on a colder snap.

Like a horse browsing along a country lane, we meander on our way. Unexpectedly as if somebody had stuck a pin into the rear on the engine, the train quickens its pace to the accompaniment of banging and clanging and rattling of buffers and chains. Presently somebody says 'This is what I call travelling' and for once we are forced to agree. There is no time for jumping off now, and as some sidings are passed, a regret is voiced that these trucks had not been left further back. On we rumble whilst the darkness rapidly closes down. The night having turned so cold, the side panels have been closed, and sitting round the bucket, gamblers included, yarns, jokes, etc., are kept going like sausages from a machine. Soon the sound of slackening speed tells us of another stoppage, but we are too interested to bother.

The train draws to a stand-still, and almost immediately the raucous voices of the N.C.O.s reach our ears. The calls are responded to by the banging of panels, and jingling of gear, mingled with roars and shouts, as everybody sorts out their own equipment. On descending we dimly see that we are on some isolated siding, with only a small points-man's cabin near at hand.

Soon we are drawn up on the road cutting the railway, and away we march, every chap seeming muckier than another, with smoke, and coal dust etc. A silent, deserted string of wagons is left behind, seen only by the fitful light of small fires, which have been dumped for safety on the permanent way. Such, dear reader, was a typical train journey of about 50 miles.

My task being now accomplished to the best of my ability, I now leave you to pass sentence being convinced, that although you have not heard my verdict, which necessitates my using the most fluent military language that I can command (and that's a lot) should you ever hear an opinion, vouched under the fore-mentioned conditions (God grant your ears may never be so offended) that your equitable justice, will ensure a leniency, due to a long suffered traveller, ungifted with the patience of Job.

Saturday 7 July 1917: The journey was resumed this morning but it finished in a different place from where we expected. The billets are very good news none-the-less. [Landrethun]

Sunday 8 July 1917: I dodged church parade this morning and was not missed. We were paid in the afternoon. I received my record (10 francs). I am on billet guard tonight.

Pay meant that all those pleasures to be found behind the line could be enjoyed to the full, baths, beer, egg and chips, universal Tommy fare, the swift production of which delicacies French and Belgian proprietors soon mastered, to their considerable profit.

This terrible war was a form of gigantic siege, the two armies in a prizefighter's embrace, a vast searing belt of devastation running like a pestilence across the line of the Western Front, by now comprising over 20,000 miles of trenches, rippling like scars. Behind, beyond the range of the guns, a hinterland of supply and troop concentration had arisen. Vast, tented cities like nomadic encampments sprang up seemingly overnight. Many locals had lost everything. For others, it was boom times:

Monday 9 July 1917: I am spending plenty of money and enjoying myself to the full. I wrote home. The weather is grand. Here we could stay for the duration.

Tuesday 10 July 1917: After dinner today I bought some cherries and now I have both diarrhoea and headache. We are going over the top soon.

Wednesday 11 July 1917: I have a touch of dysentery now and I can't eat. We were practising for the attack today. It was warm work.

Thursday 12 July 1917: We were practicing [*sic*] again today. I'm feeling worse. I've eaten nothing since dinner on Tuesday when I ate the cherries. I'll go to the doctor tomorrow.

Maintaining the general health of the army was an Olympian task. War inevitably spurs progress on medical science but trench-living is a hygienist's nightmare: trench foot, lice, dysentery and, most fearfully, typhus (which had stalked armies since ever the first one marched) were constant fears:

Friday 13 July 1917: I went to the doctor this morning and was excused duty. I'm feeling pretty bad. I did billet guard tonight.

Saturday 14 July 1917: I was at the doctor again today and was excused duty again. I'm feeling a little better.

Sunday 15 July 1917: I dodged church parade this morning although I'm almost ashamed to own it but I have bound myself to tell the exact truth and nothing but the truth.

Monday 16 July 1917: The attack was practised again today. As we are leaving tomorrow we are having a singsong tonight.

Tuesday 17 July 1917: The singsong went well last night but I'm afraid I didn't shine. However I was determined to retrieve my reputation. I sang about two lines when the orderly sergeant ordered the affair to cease as it was after lights out. It is a lovely day but too warm for marching. We are all packed up waiting for the fall in. After a short but tiring march we got motors. In these we travelled for miles. At the journey's end we were like bakers with dust. My hair being white I was like Uncle Tom. [Dickebusche]

For all these youthful Hectors who'd ventured across the Channel their expectation that the damsels of France and Belgium would be lining up to surrender their favours proved an illusion. Tommy found the forward areas devoid of females and those he met in lanes and billets to the rear proved less than glamorous. Their only likely contact would be the ritual squalor of the red lamp area:

Wednesday 18 July 1917: We are resting today so we are doing nothing. I'm expecting a letter from home soon. I hope I shall get it before we leave for the trenches on Friday.

Thursday 19 July 1917: News has come that Jerry expects us to attack so he is massing his men and guns on our part of the front to receive us so the attack is put back. We are moving down again tomorrow. [Steenvoorde]

Friday 20 July 1917: Our new billets were reached early in the afternoon. It's all right. I hope we are paid tomorrow. I've had no letter yet but there is less hurry now.

Saturday 21 July 1917/Sunday 22 July 1917: I awoke with a sore head yesterday and I felt absolutely rotten. While the Company was paraded before the colonel I turned sick and had to be taken from the ranks. I was just as bad after dinner so I was excused parade. Today I don't feel quite so bad but I've an awful sore head. I was cheered up considerably when we were paraded for pay. I'll have a good time before I leave this town. I have entered the battalion sports which come off tomorrow.

The momentum for Haig's summer offensive was building. The unaccountable delay between Plumer's success at Messines in June and the launch of Haig's grand summer offensive had not only allowed the Germans respite but the weather had turned:

Monday 23 July 1917: I arose fine and fit this morning. The day was glorious and the sports were a great success. My company carried off their share of the honours. I was running grand in the sack race but alas my legs got mixed up and down I went in a heap with some fellows on top of me. I enjoyed myself never-the-less and ended the day happily.

Tuesday 24 July 1917: A move is being made for the trenches tomorrow. I'm still sweating on a letter from home. Warning for the trenches was read out this evening [Dickebusche]. The penalty of desertion from now is death.

Rain and the mud it produced would be the lingering memory of the Third Battle of Ypres, a terrible grinding attrition slogged out in nightmare conditions. Lloyd George would brand his commander in chief as a 'military Moloch' (one who demanded a continual blood sacrifice):

Wednesday 25 July 1917: It has been raining all day but it cleared up unexpectedly in the evening. I received a letter this evening. We were all ready with tents struck and everything ready to move off when suddenly the order was cancelled. I suppose we start tomorrow instead.

Thursday 26 July 1917: I wrote home today and was in such a hurry to catch the post that I forgot to put in a silk P.C. [post-card] that I bought so I shall have to carry it into this attack. I don't think we shall shift until tomorrow.

Friday 27 July 1917: We went for a route march but were back for dinner. We are not moving.

Saturday 28 July 1917/Sunday 29 July 1917: We shifted yesterday but on arrival it was too dark to write the diary. The walking was so hot that our clothes and even equipment were wet with sweat. We had to lie down in these wet things.

To sleep was impossible. The guns and shells were banging and whizzing wholesale. Jerry sent over gas so we were up all night with our gas helmets on. The rain came down mercilessly in the afternoon completely soaking us. We shift again tonight.

The eve of battle was approaching:

Monday 30 July 1917: I am now back in the trenches again. Jerry is shelling like mad. We go to the front line tonight and over the top in the morning. My thoughts are mixed and unsettled at present and I can't say I'm feeling too brave but it has to be done so the sooner the better as this shelling is getting on my nerves. I think I'll come through all right at least I'll try to return for my parcel from home. These trenches are knee deep in mud and a drizzly rain has been on all day so it's pretty miserable. The rum came round this evening. My supply fairly warmed me up and it put new life into me. We move up tonight and over at dawn so here's luck.

4

THE VETERAN

Haig had a grand plan. The offensive would involve a left and right hook. One axis of advance would clear the high ground to the east of Ypres, lost in 1914, and reach as far as Passchendaele. The other would be a giant bound for the sea, for the Channel coast, where the menace of the U-Boats could be eliminated, the attack coinciding with an amphibious assault.

Cannily, the commander-in-chief had warned his political masters that even if this bold strategy was not wholly successful, the offensive would draw the enemy into a grinding battle of attrition, sucking in his precious reserves. This was nearer the mark. Whether Haig seriously believed in a final breakthrough may be open to question. Attrition, that deadly game of profit and loss, would be the real objective. The doctrine, given prevailing circumstances, was strategically sound, even inevitable. For the poor bloody infantry it spelt untold suffering and anguish:

Tuesday 31 July 1917: We were over this morning and I saw sights that I never saw before or wish to see again. It was terrible yet it was wonderful. I will not attempt to describe the sights, sounds and feelings that I saw, heard, and felt because it would be impossible. I got through without a scratch. (The Battle of Pilckem [Ridge])

The Battle of Pilckem Ridge was to be the curtain-raiser. As previously mentioned, General Hugh 'Paddy' Gough would be attacking along a frontage of some 14,000yd from Klein Zillebeke in the south, to the line of the Ypres–Staden Railway in the north. He would throw nine divisions and one brigade into the battle plus two French divisions in support on the northerly flank. The attack was to be proceeded by a massive artillery drenching. Gough's plan was more ambitious than Plumer's. Haig felt Gough's cavalry elan was what was needed, even though Fifth Army staff and planning were far below the standard of Second Army:

> Everybody was miserable and grousey. The night had been one continual gas attack, so gas helmets had been worn throughout. To make matters worse, the rain had poured mercilessly in the afternoon. It was the 29th July 1917 and we were lying on the outskirts of Dickebusch, waiting to move up to go over the top in a day or two hence. The ground being low lying soon became a mass of mud and slime. The small bivouac tents were poor shelters from the drenching downpour. Under such conditions no fires could possibly be lighted. All that day we squatted under our low tents, wet, and miserable, so that when orders came to prepare to move we were glad to have something to do.
>
> At the appointed time we 'fell in' and muddy and weary as we were we started forward, with the slow ponderous movement so common with the expeditionary force. The roads were calf deep with mud, while the rest of the country was half lake, half quagmire. Frequently the enemy shells would land in the near vicinity with sudden slaps and mud showers, so that we had a mud bath every now and then. Dead animals and disabled wagons lay scattered in profusion. In many cases these objects were almost buried in the boggy terrain.

Gough's plan called for a series of attacks, all aimed at punching through the crust of German defences, then moving on to their second ('Albrecht') and finally third ('Wilhelm') lines. Further exploitation towards the fourth line would be determined by local successes and opportunities presented. Some 120 tanks were to be deployed in the assault, with 48 more in reserve:

> At last we came to a corduroy road that is a roadway of tree trunks, which was also plentifully dotted with deceased mules and timber wagons. This road was the stopping place for the transport evidently and some of them had stopped for good. We turned along this road and slipping and stumbling over the wet logs, we made our way cursing and grousing until we came upon our own transport wagons waiting to be unloaded. At this point we left the road to the right and cut across what had at one time been fields, but was now a dismal stretch of slime, sparsely dotted with distorted tree stumps.
>
> It was almost dark by this time, but the rain had eased off to a fine drizzle. We made for some tree trunks that ran across our front, about a couple of hundred yards away. On reaching our landmark, we saw that the trunks were followed by a communication trench and into this trench we filed.
>
> Now a communication trench has no fire-step or dugouts, that is, if it has been dug for a communication trench. This trench had neither, therefore and what is more, any duckboards that had not been blown away, were either so badly broken as to be a danger to unwary feet, or had sunk so far in the muddy bottom as to be absolutely out of commission. The sides of the trench were of such a shifting nature, that frames of wire netting were required to hold them up. The least touch caused the slime to ooze through the netting. The bottom was on an average covered by a foot of water. Plainly speaking what was being misnamed a trench, was only a common ditch.

In the dry season I should say it would be about six feet deep, at this time it was anything from seven feet. There being no-where to sit, I took up my stand right on the corner shown in the sketch in the diary [Zillebeke Lake]. I had hardly placed my rifle in the driest position I could find, before a corporal ordered me to follow him. When I got out of the old trench, I found that quite a few had followed the corporal besides me.

This time it was anticipated the guns would destroy the German wire, knock out their outposts and provide effective counter-battery fire. All this would be needed. In the breathing space since their wake-up call at Messines the Germans had been busy. They were very quick learners.

As John Buchan observed, gone was the old system of linear trenches. Now there was a bristling grid, studded with strong-points. The German front line was a dense belt of bunkers and fortified ruins, all with interlocking fields of fire. It was lightly held, primarily by machine-gunners. Their Flanders Line was probably the most complex and brilliant series of fortifications since Hadrian's Wall. Arthur and his comrades were about to take it on and go in by the front door. Tommy was not privy to his commander's wider strategy. Moving up into the line was a nightmare in itself:

Anyhow we all continued to follow our leader and we soon found ourselves at the transport wagons. It then dawned on me that we had clicked for a fatigue party. Ah well thought I, now I'm here I'll make the best of it and I selected a sack of jam. These needed less careful handling and all true soldiers always keep an eye for the main chance. Before I regained the ditch, one of the pots of jam was mine, this I resolved to keep for future use.

All that night we stood in the drizzle soaked through and through and scarcely exchanging a word. Each man seemed busy with his own thoughts of home and the morrow. As another dreary day dawned, the drizzle was replaced by a very damp unpleasant mist. The German guns had shelled our vicinity rather heavily, but we suffered no casualties.

Now like kittens in a box we became restless as the day advanced, and we wanted to explore our surroundings. First one jumped out of the ditch, then another jumped out and soon we were all out. It was when I clambered out that I saw Zillebeke Lake for the first time. Reference to the sketch gives a better idea than I could by writing. The darkness again closed down upon us, bringing fresh supplies of rain, and we longed for the attack even if only to relieve our monotony. The water in our ditch had risen considerably but we thought it better to stand in it than out on top getting the icy wind that was blowing.

About 9 p.m. an officer and a sergeant came wading along issuing out rum rations, and warning us to be ready to move about midnight. Hither-to I had refused my rations of rum but this night I would have supped with the devil himself if I could have bettered my case by doing so. Rum rations at the best were never of generous proportions, but as we were all fairly well knocked up, the ration on this occasion was passable. Mine I know did wonders for me.

At last through the darkness and rain, word was passed back to prepare to move. Wearily and stiffly, but with sighs of relief we slung our rifles and hitched our belts, and got ready for the fray. After a short delay we started forward, to what, we knew not, but we hoped for the best.

The night was now pitch black but the rain had ceased. On we went, a grim crowd in single file, moving along the intricate trenches like a gigantic reptile wriggling through an enormous crooked tube. Word was constantly being passed back of 'tricky duckboards, and missing duckboards', but on we laboriously splashed and waded. There wasn't a man of us who was not encased in mud but I have to admit even if it is dirty it certainly keeps the heat in and the cold out.

The German artillery kept up a desultory action, but he was registering too close for our comfort. As we proceeded the effects of the gun-fire were becoming more apparent to us. The trenches were taking on a more battered look, and the dead men lying in them were getting more numerous as we went forward. The constant cry now was 'Shaky duckboard here. Mind this dead man, be careful there's no duckboard here.'

The trenches soon had been so badly shelled that in some places we were walking in the open, where big shell holes had taken the place of that bit of trench. In the still surviving lengths of trench, the dead men were often so numerous that it was impossible to proceed without walking on them.

This section of trenches was awful. One moment we were wading up to our middles in water the next we were wobbling and balancing over the bodies of our unfortunate comrades. Now the word was being passed from the rear, 'Go slow in front; halt in front,' as somebody got stuck losing those in front, and holding up those behind. That journey was like a nightmare. Even yet as I write this I can fancy I see the gruesome forms lying in the flooded craters by the fitful green lights, of the Verey lights, which reflected on the ink black water, casting an opalescent glow on the ghastly faces.

Zero hour was fixed at 0350 hours, in theory this was break of day but low cloud caused a lingering darkness. The attack would be preceded by a rolling barrage (this was a form of continuous artillery support where the guns pummelled enemy ground ahead in a series of timed 'lifts'):

There was no time nor was this the place to be sentimental, and we were hurried forward to be in our positions by 2 a.m., the appointed time for the kick-off. Through time we arrived amongst a jumbled mass of sand bags, sheet iron, wooden supports, and planks, rifles, equipment and dead bodies. This had been our front line. We crossed over this shambles, and being now in no man's land we advanced about thirty yards.

In whispers we were sorted out into our proper sections, and thus we got the order to kneel. We were then divided into small groups as the diary sketch shows [The Barrage]. The enemy guns still played on our front line, but the poor chaps who held it now were beyond the consequences of modern warfare, and our glorious dead lay with a supreme indifference, unattainable outside the realms of immortality.

As we knelt there waiting the command of our officer, who constantly gazed at his wrist-watch with the sheet of blackness before us, and the German curtain fire behind us, roaring in its seeming impatience, my thoughts were strangely far distant from the battlefield.

I wondered if I was in the thoughts of somebody at that precise moment. Then came a wave of pride. Here was I among men sharing the risks and uncertainties of being in the very front ranks of the empire, against its enemies. My patriotism was strong in my breast then, and as a youth will do I began to dream of what might be. Would a great chance come my way, if so, would I make the best of it. Of course I would, I am a man now, a real man thought I.

Then the tiny grim imp of stern reality slowly inserted his prong of cold reason, and like a flash I saw again our front line and its occupants. Perhaps they too had dreamed, but reality had shattered their castles. Oh my God! Would the supports who would follow in our tracks find me mangled and torn, gazing into the great beyond. Ugh! The thoughts sent the cold sweat from my brow. Oh this waiting is worse than a hundred deaths. Heavens, will the order never come?

This was the testing moment for each and every man. The final test of battle for which every soldier trains and yet many might have hoped would never come:

For want of action my highly strung nerves were straining to breaking point. Whizz! Shhh! Crash! Bang! Boom-Boom! Boom! 'Forward men,' calmly said our officer. Thank heaven I breathed as I rose to move forward. That order saved me. I had been allowed to brood too long. This statement may sound strange if not ridiculous, but during my active service days, my one worry was, I was frightened that I should become afraid.

The barrage from our guns fell about fifty yards ahead, exactly at 2 a.m. on our part of the front; for a few minutes it shattered, and battered the German front line, then it roared forward. The sketch in the diary shows my impression, which I kept of the sight. It was as if the earth had opened in half and vomited forth flames and sparks of gorgeous rich colours.

Ypres Salient had scarcely moved in three years of bitter fighting. This relatively constricted area had been turned into a shell scarred, mud garnished wasteland, a vision of the abyss:

the constant shelling had turned the country into a state of indescribable desolation. There was scarcely an inch that was not shell-pocked, not a house stood, nor a tree stump more than a few feet high. There was nothing green to be seen anywhere.

Movement was nearly as fraught in darkness as it was in daylight. The night sky was lit up Guy Fawkes style by the criss-cross tracers of German flares, hanging like demonic fireflies. Random, long range machine-gun fire claimed many casualties as men struggled up through the dank maze of communication trenches. It rained yet again all though 30 July:

> The ground was in an awful miry state, but we had not squelched forward very far before three or four prisoners came up to us unarmed and with hands held high. Our officer obtained what information he could, but the corporal treated them as guardedly as if they had been bristling with guns. It did not hinder him from searching them thoroughly however.

The 30th Division's primary objective was to get across Gheluvelt Plateau as far as Glencorse Wood:

> We had no time to lose, so we hurried on as best we could, but with the boggy ground, and the detours we had to make round small lakes, our barrage soon thundered away into the distance, leaving us hopelessly behind. The section about thirty yards on our right, received a heavy German shell right in their midst. Shortly afterwards, I saw one of the tanks in front of us catch fire. I think by the blaze it must have been a supply tank.
>
> The enemy pestered us with a slow but annoying fire of 5-9 [inch] shells, and an assortment of small shells. As we plunged on, one of our section who was walking at my left shoulder suddenly collapsed with a sigh. A splinter had struck him in the abdomen. Some stretcher bearers were following our party, but before they came up the poor chap had expired.
>
> It was afterwards it was remarked, that during the previous day, the unfortunate man had been very reticent in his speech and actions. Strict orders had been issued before the battle, that nobody but stretcher bearers were to stop for wounded,

also that no water bottles or bandages were to be used except for personal use. We therefore after a sympathetic glance pushed on, besides it might be anybody's turn next.

The Battalion war diary confirms the difficult nature of the night approach. It was 1230 hours by the time A and B Companies began to move up towards their start line from Wellington Crescent, with C Company and Battalion HQ following on. Zero Hour was nearly there by the time the men clambered into the scrapes in no man's land. Cohesion had already begun to suffer, company commanders were not fully in touch with their individual platoons.

For the actual assault, 90th Brigade would deploy 18th Manchesters on the right, supported by 2nd RSF, 16th and 17th Manchesters on the left; 18th and 16th Manchesters were to reach and secure the 'Blue Line', 2nd RSF would then pass through to attain the 'Black Line'. A third objective, the 'Green Line', was assigned to another formation. Twenty-first Brigade would attack on the right of 90th Brigade. The battalion was deployed in three waves: A Company in the first wave was to assault two strong-points located on the 'Black Line', B Company was to take the trenches in front of the line within and north of Inverness Copse. The third wave would comprise both C and D Companies, who were to take and hold the remainder of the 'Black Line'.

In theory this was all practicable but, as ever in trench warfare, few plans survived contact with reality – the black, shell-ripped morass over which the infantrymen were expected to advance. Beyond Jackdaw Support trench it got worse. As ever, the creeping barrage sailed majestically ahead. Both A and B Companies lost direction, working too far to the left. By the time Arthur and his comrades reached Jackdaw Reserve, they were an hour behind schedule, their barrage lost in the smoke-shrouded desolation ahead of them.

It was 0600 hours by the time the battalion moved off beyond the Blue Line and, within thirty minutes they were pinned down by enemy fire, a mere 200yd further on. Casualties were heavy:

It was now daylight. Heavy black clouds clustered in the sky, while a driving drizzle was quickly turning the boggy earth into a series of large lakes of water, through which rising pieces of mud appeared like tiny islands.

For weeks before the attack we had been instructed on a model battlefield, as to the various directions we were to take in getting to our objective which was termed the black line. Well to tell the truth, even with the photographic birds-eye views of the real battlefields, I could not really grasp how we were going to carry out such niceties in the face of enemy fire and finish up on the black-line according to plan. Anyhow the headquarters' staff seemed to think the plan would work so as a consequence we started off in one direction, then we suddenly swung sharply to the right, then some yards further on we turned half left, and I'm sure we covered nearly a mile before we even saw a trench.

By the railway Embankment C Company had netted a haul of half a hundred prisoners and a brace of Maxims. But their inspirational officer Captain J.B. Orr was killed there as they were digging in. B Company (Captain D.H. Kennedy MC) also took a couple of dozen captives while storming Stirling Castle. The attack by 21st Brigade on the right had stalled short of the Blue Line, so the RSF battalion's flank was 'in the air'. A reserve brigade, the 89th, attempted to come up but was held up short of the Blue Line:

At last we dropped into one and the first thing I saw was an officer lying dead with a handkerchief over his face, and his servant collecting his books and papers. Now we were in the enemy trenches, our work commenced. We had carried our sacks of bombs a long way and they were heavy so we thought the sooner we delivered them the sooner would we lighten our load.

The dead officer made us more merciless than we otherwise would have been, so we went along that trench and every dugout we came to we flung in a bomb or two then called on the occupants to come out. The mills bomb goes off five seconds after the pin strikes the cap. We held it for three seconds while by the time we shouted four seconds had elapsed so that the Jerry down below usually stayed there.

One of the major limitations in successful offensive action was caused by the simple fact that communications had not caught up with gunnery. There was no tactical radio. Arthur and his fellows, struggling to maintain their advance, had to watch the creeping barrage moving inexorably forward by pre-arranged lifts, marching on into a diminishing fury:

Our wonderful barrage had driven most of the enemy below, but as I have already said, owing to our slow progress it had out-distanced us. Had the ground been any way good we would have kept behind the barrage and caught old Fritz in his dugouts, but whilst we were floundering along slowly he had time to emerge from his holes and hence we were faced with a difficult task.

With our protecting barrage long since rumbling in the distance we were now exposed to the German machine-gunners. Under their withering fire our sections were soon dispersed. We would be ploughing forward when suddenly the stutter of a machine-gun and the vicious swish of bullets would send us rolling into the nearest shell hole invariably half full of water.

In a short time officers were without men, and men were
without officers. Bombers and grenadiers and Lewis-gunners,
and rifle men, were all mixed up. Some parties consisted of
nearly all N.C.O.s, while other parties didn't have even one.
Nevertheless, forward was the order of the day and mixed up
as we were in parties of threes and fours and in some cases a
dozen we moved on always being broken up by the gunners.
Sometimes I was alone when a sudden dive for safety would
land me among a party.

All in all 30th Division's attack was soon stalling in the horri-
ble wet ground. There was confusion in the dark and murk of
battle, flayed by the lethal dirge of those many German machine
guns which had survived bombardment. Mid-morning saw
18th Division begin to filter through the brigade positions,
their objective being the Green Line. Their attack fell about a
100yd short of the ground won by B and C Companies. On
the left, their progress was better, advancing some 200yd beyond
the embankment. In these circumstances the survivors of B
Company were obliged to fall back to the Blue Line:

Things were fast assuming proportions of a hopeless muddle,
because not only were sections disorganised, and mixed up
but whole battalions were being involved. Due credit must
be and will be, by me, given to the German rearguard, who
held us up that day. It was certain death for them because our
waves of infantry had got between them in most cases and
their main body while to expose themselves was to draw the
fire of us chaps who were looking for them. Like the heroes
they were they fought like tigers, withdrawing from crater to
crater as we steadily, but very slowly pushed on.

At approximately 1400 hours the Germans unleashed a deluge of fire which rained down for a full six hours. The Fusiliers clung to their gains but at considerable cost. At 1700 hours orders had been given for 90th Brigade to retire, but only half the troops dug-in received the message, the rest hung on through the night. Even once they'd withdrawn to Zillebeke Lake trench, the survivors were still within range of the German guns. In all, the battalion suffered 208 casualties:

> Yes these enemy gunners sold themselves dearly and so harassed and broken by their deadly fire were we, that our position was a mystery to us. At length I found myself going forward with a lance corporal and two privates of my own battalion, and a couple of chaps of a Manchester battalion. We could see none of our own troops near us now and as we happened on a German trench that was wicker lined and had at least a semblance of dryness we dropped in, and prepared to hold on till such time as we could reconnect ourselves with another body of our comrades.
>
> The skies were very lowering and grey-black clouds raced across them and the drizzle had turned to sheets of rain and the mist in the distance was thickening but the stutter of Lewis and machine-guns came to our ears through the awful weather. Occasional bursts of rifle fire now plain now faint reached us also. The artillery seemed to have given up the contest on both sides.
>
> As I peeped over the enemy's parodos, all I could see was big sheets of water, reflecting the sullen skies, all lashed by the heavy rain, while here and there lay a body soaked and sodden and muddy. The enemy armoured planes were flying backwards, and forward, about twelve feet above the parapet, giving out bursts of machine-gun fire.

All momentum and cohesion was now lost. As the battle unfolded and the ability of senior officers, from brigade through to division and corps level, to influence events waned, the fight became a soldier's battle, few being aware of what was happening beyond their own section or platoon, company at best:

> The energy seemed to have gone from the attack, but our slow advance owing firstly to the weather and secondly to the plucky enemy machine-gunners, had allowed the German resistance to stiffen. We hung on in our position waiting to either get in touch with the enemy or our own troops, but preferably the latter.
>
> It was well on in the day when a party came plunging along with news that the relief was in position. Whether the relief was in front or behind I did not know and I suppose now I shall never know. Trusting the bad light to protect us, we climbed out on top of the trench, and joined our new companions. On we waded and sprawled when we came to a guide tape-line. This white tape, it was anything but white now, had been laid to guide troops to a dressing post. To cut a story short we followed the white tape and reached the post.

War is a surprisingly lonely business. Even with the huge forces deployed most soldiers would not yet have glimpsed an enemy, except perhaps for dead, wounded or prisoners. Battlefields often appear very much a blank canvas to participants. There is never any room for complacency. Nonetheless, sticking your head up above the parapet was always inadvisable:

> After many enquiries we found ourselves at our battalion gathering place. A wretched night was spent in some dugouts in a wood. The next day parties were told off to do duty as

stretcher bearers. The party I was with was to carry wounded from a subterranean post to some ruins called Dormie House. The post was a fair distance from the house and it was no joke wading knee deep in mud with one corner of a stretcher on your shoulder.

Some German guns were playing on our quarter, and the job was made perfectly nerve breaking. Several times the shell fire stopped the work, but it was in the evening that I was separated from my party. The weather was still dirty and no signs of improvement could be seen. As the sketch shows one of our guns had been put out of action near the house and I think Jerry was firing at it not knowing of its plight. Anyway that gun had to be passed by us going to and from the post to the house.

Under such conditions, we were quite fed up and personally speaking, I for one had reached the stage that I cared little what happened. There was mud on nearly every square inch of me. The last issue of rations I had received had been three days before, at Zillebeke Lake. Since then my iron rations, and that purloined pot of jam had been my only subsistence.

Nearly all the party was in a similar way. It was during one of Jerry's short sharp vicious bombardments that I lost the party or perhaps the party lost me. I didn't know. I didn't care. I simply got my head under cover and waited. On emerging from the mud I couldn't see a soul, but I was so tired that I don't suppose I could have noticed anybody a few yards off. Aimlessly I wandered about and at last more by chance than anything else I stumbled among the ruins of Dormie House.

The R.A.M.C. men who were in charge of this dispatch post had been smelling the rum jar oftener than was wise for them informed me that all working parties had departed for the night. I secured my rifle from a niche where I had placed it and somewhat lighter-hearted I set out to get back to our starting point. Along the masses of communication trenches I plodded a lonely soul on a lonely landscape.

The BEF had, on 31 July, advanced an average of 3,000yd at a cost of 30,000 casualties. German losses were probably very similar. Half of Gough's tanks were out of action and then there was the rain. Down it came in unending sheets of soaking misery turning the wet ground into a swamp:

> It was still raining. By this time dear reader, you must have observed that this is a story of rain and mud but I defy your imagination unless you have been to the places of which I write under the same conditions, to fully comprehend the amount of rain and mud that was bestowed on that part of the world.

Wet and filthy, cloying, sucking, deadly mud; the new arbiter of battle. Industry could produce ever more terrible weapons but could not halt the incessant rain:

> At length I left the trenches and arriving at our old camp – it was deserted. Judge of the depths of misery in which I was again cast! I was tired, footsore, weary and hungry and mucky. It was darkening and no-body was in sight. I knew not which way to turn to find friends but seeing a line of stumps through the murk I concluded that they indicated a road. I got on to the road anyway. If I stopped one person for information I stopped a dozen but one seemed to contradict the other while some who had no idea of what I asked just said anything. Yes a soldier may be as welcome as the flowers in May with his own mob, but others help very little a strayed comrade of another battalion.
>
> Throughout the dark dirty night I doggedly splashed about and the dull grey wet morning found me dreamily plodding,

God knows where? I remember walking towards a cluster of tents and timber-wagons. The next thing I mind was [*sic*] I was half lying against a wagon with the rain beating on my face and my own section officer giving me a good drink of rum.

Everybody was pleased to see me but I took most to the post corporal for he had a parcel and a letter for me as the diary states. It also states that I attacked the parcel. Well I not only attacked it but I demolished it. The letter had to wait for like a pig that has been fed I rolled over and my thick coating of mud helped to keep me warm while I slept.

This narrative has been stretched over a period of five days, from 29th July 1917 to 2nd August 1917. It is the best I can do as regards describing my experiences before, during and after the struggle of might and endurance, known as … The Third Battle of Ypres.

In the early fighting, gains were made though these were modest when measured against losses. Over such dreadful ground, tanks were of little value, constantly getting bogged down and offering target practice for German gunners. Attacks continued through August though the ghastly weather continued. Colonel Von Lossberg's defences proved a very tough nut indeed and, by the end of August, Fifth Army had lost some 60,000 men.

When the burden was shifted from the Fifth to the Second Army, Plumer was to focus on the Gheluvelt Plateau. As at Messines, 'Daddy' Plumer had thought long and hard about the tactical problem. His artillery would be both sledgehammer and scalpel, while still providing a shield for the infantry. Their main assault would be preceded by trained skirmishers, the basis of infiltration tactics. Attacks would proceed on a local 'bite and hold' basis, a pause between each bound for consolidation and allowing fresh units to pass through. Reserves would always be on hand to reinforce success. That at least was the hope.

A treasure trove of all the contents of 'the box in the attic'.

28384 Private Roberts, 3rd Battalion KOSB.

Arthur's parents – David Roberts and Laura Dann.

41880 Private Roberts, 2nd Battalion R.S.F.

Arthur playing in Glasgow's British Legion Dance Band.

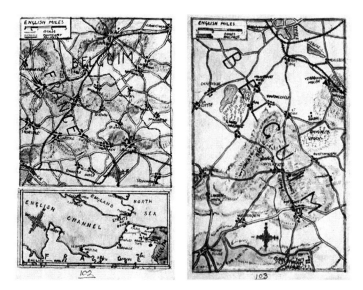

Above left: Map of France and Belgium, beautifully drawn by Arthur.

Above right: Another beautifully drawn map by Arthur, this time of the Wytschaete/Messines area in Belgium, the main areas of Haig's operations in the summer and autumn of 1917.

SS *King Edward*, 'The Leave-boat'.

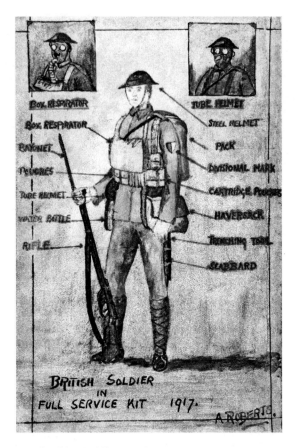

British soldier in full service kit.

Left: 'Trench Duty': watercolour from 'The Memoirs'; Right: 'Railway Dump' watercolour.

'Reserves near Neuve Église' watercolour.

'Zillebeke Lake' watercolour. The trench seen in the picture, which runs around the lake, was where C and D Company spent the night preparatory to the advance, which was the commencement of the Third Battle of Ypres, 31 July 1917.

'Gordon Road' watercolour. 'This road runs from "Suicide Corner" in Kemmel to "Fifteen Inch Corner" in Wycheate [*sic*]. The Labour Corps had a constant job keeping it in repair. The enemy had a fair view of it so mats were put up along the most exposed parts as shown in the picture. "Lamp Post Corner" is also on this road.'

'Wytschaete' watercolour. 'The picture shows all that was left of the village when I last saw it about the 25th August 1917. Just a few yards past the standing ruin is "Fifteen Inch Corner". It is called that because right at the side of the crossroads is a big German 15-in shell that has failed to explode. By gum, if it had exploded, I don't suppose there would have been any ruins lying or standing.'

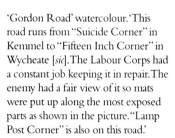

LEFT Edinburgh . . 19 May 1917
ARRIVED AT Boulogne . . 20 "
" Etaples . T. 21-3 June
" Poperinghe . R. 4-8
" Ypres . S.&F.L. 9-15
" Dickebusche RSV. 16-21
" Journehem . R. 22-26
" MARCHING . 27
" Dickebusche RSV 28-5 July
" MARCHING . 6
" Landrethun .R. 7-14
" Dickebusche RSV 17-20
" Steenvoorde R. 21-24
" Dickebusche RSV 24-28
" Zillebeke Lake S. 29-30
IN ACTION. . 31-2 Aug
RESTING . . 3
" Selvister Capel R. 4-6
" Caestre . R. 7-9
" Berthen . R 10-21
" Kemmel . RSV. 22-29

T. Training | RSV. Reserves | GD. Guard Duty
R. Resting | STD. Stationary | OL. On Leave
S. Supports | FL. Front Line | TRAV. Travelling

ARRIVED AT Neuve Eglise. RSV. 30-2 Sept 1917
" Kemmel . RSV. 3-10
" Wytschaete FL&S. 11-21
" St Eloi RSV. 22-27
" Lindenhoek RSV. 28-11 Oct
" Dranoutre HOSPITAL 11-16
" Kemmel . RSV. 16-17
" Wytschaete . FL. 18-20
" Kemmel . RSV. 21-27
" Bailleul. TRAV. 27-28
" Etaples . GD. 28-4 Dec
" Le Havre. STD. 5-21 Feb 1918
" Glasgow. OL. 22-6 March

Arthur's travels.

YPRES — MENIN

'Hell's Fire or Shrapnel Corner' watercolour.

Watercolour depicting the opening barrage at the start of the Third Battle of Ypres.

'Frontline near Wycheate [*sic*]' watercolour.

'Ypres': a watercolour from 'The Memoirs'.

'Zillebeke 1917' watercolour.

'Dickebusche Lake and Chateau Segard' watercolour.

'Dormie House' watercolour.

Clockwise from above: Jack Moran: 'Considered a likely lad. He is an amateur from the cottonopolis. A very nice chap and would be real hot stuff if he were not so fond of the gay life. However before he went home he pulled up considerably'; The Water Tower: 'This tower supplied water to the camp independent to the French supply. It is between 90 and 100 feet high. Except workmen I was the only person who mounted it. I used to enjoy lying up there on a warm day with my camera as a book.'; Bert Tilney: 'Another good lad of the camp and a good all round sportsman. A bit sure of his accomplishments perhaps, but a fine chap never the less. He comes from Newcastle I believe.'

British military prison: 'This view was taken from the top of the water tower. In the middle distance can be seen the prison.'

French shipyard: 'This is another tower top picture. The ship seen on the stocks is the 'Charhonier' and I had the pleasure of seeing her launched.'

Royal Engineer workshops: 'Another tower top picture showing the workshops. Most of the work here was done by German prisoners. The hut in the fore-ground is O.C.'s office and the Company office.'

'This is an interior view of an R.E. sports hut. At the other side of the ring is the suspended punch ball. To the left of that are the rings. The box to the left is for gloves, dumbbells, clubs, rings, towels, basins etc ...'

'This is a room of an officer whom I looked after. He was called Major Bliss and he remained in blissful ignorance of the trouble I used to have with his big, swell carpet.'

A sleeping hut: 'An interior view of the inside of a hut I occupied. In the foreground is the chair left behind by the barber … the barber's chair in John Bull could never tell a yarn that this chair could if it could speak.'

A sand blower: 'The River Seine about here has a very sandy bottom; consequently dredgers are always at work to keep the harbour clear.'

A canal.

A village rendez-vous: 'Many a good night's dancing, drinking, debating etc. have I spent in this café. A crowd of us used to frequent it nightly and the musicians made money and so did the girls, on the quiet!'

'Me Again'.

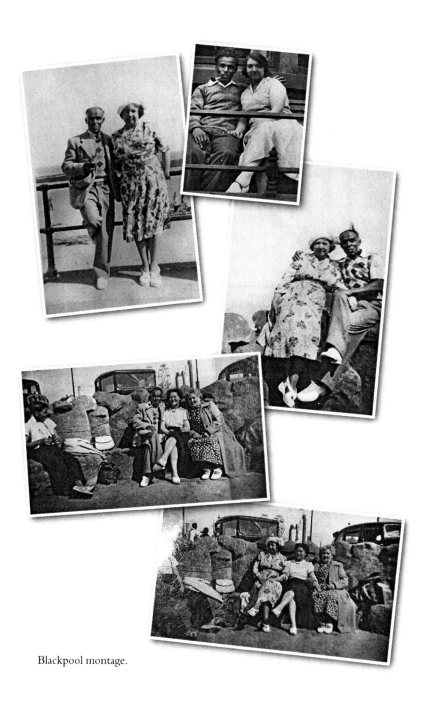

Blackpool montage.

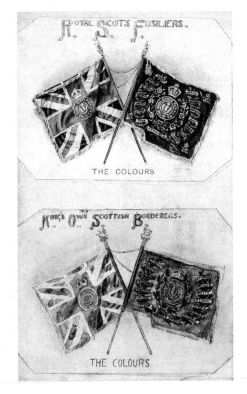

The colours.

5

THE SURVIVOR

Wednesday 1 August 1917: I did work as stretcher bearer today. It was pretty rotten for one of my temperament. We shift back tonight.

Thursday 2 August 1917: I got separated from my party last night so I came staggering into camp today covered with mud and soaked to the skin. I received a good rum issue however as I was just about done not having had food for a couple of days. Shortly after the post corporal gave me a parcel and a letter from home. I immediately attacked the parcel after which I slept some hours. The weather is rotten and the roads ankle deep in mud.

Being a stretcher bearer was no sinecure, the work was dangerous and exhausting. Regimental aid posts were provided near to the front line but could usually only cope with the walking wounded. Those more seriously injured would have to be stretchered back to the dressing station. Many never made it; nor, all too often, did their bearers:

Friday 3 August 1917: Early this morning Jerry lobbed over a few shells but they did little or no damage. Motors took us down the line a bit before dinner. Dinner was served on arrival. The weather is bad and is hampering the advance which we started. We have pitched tents so we shall stay here a little while.

Saturday 4 August 1917: Orders came to move so we harnessed up and walked for our train. After a short train journey which took a long while we arrived at a station from which we walked umpteen kilometres. Our billets are much to our liking [Silvestre Capel].

Already the unending rain of that soaked Flanders summer was making the battlefield impassable. The Third Battle of Ypres would become synonymous with mud; a quaking, shifting morass of repellent gas-garnished slime that could swallow men whole:

Sunday 5 August 1917: We rested today. A memorial service took place in the village in honour of the men who fell in action. I wrote home today. A new pair of boots was supplied to me this afternoon.

Monday 6 August 1917: The weather is clearing up and we are clearing out tomorrow.

Tuesday 7 August 1917: Our new billets were reached before dinner. They are just as good as the ones we've left. I received another letter from home today. I think it is time we were looking for a pay [Caestre].

The soldier's lot is not to reflect, at least not at the time. The everyday necessities of his life, even the humdrum, bond him further into the communal weft of his unit. Where battalions were regularly decimated by the great, insatiable mincer of the front, survivors were always needed to facilitate rebuilding:

Wednesday 8 August 1917: Parading started today again. Pay has not arrived yet.

Thursday 9 August 1917: I was painting transport wagons today. Another shift is expected tomorrow; still no pay.

Friday 10 August 1917: We have arrived. This is a better place and we are in tents. Pay is still missing [Berthen].

Saturday 11 August 1917: As I was on billet guard, I escaped rouse parade.

Sunday 12 August 1917: I attended church service this morning, the first time for weeks. It was an open air one with a brass band. A jolly fine service and our pay has come at last. I received my record (15 francs). What a time I had it was glorious.

Pay and prayer both of great comfort, especially when they arrive together! Out of the line, the war could seem very distant:

Monday 13 August 1917: We were at the range today. I went to see a concert party called the 'Blue Birds' this evening.

Tuesday 14 August 1917: I visited the 'Blue Birds' again this evening.

Wednesday 15 August 1917: The General inspected us today. I received a letter from home. I saw the 'Blue Birds' again this evening.

Thursday 16 August 1917: There were the ordinary parades this morning. The weather is glorious.

Friday 17 August 1917: A bathing parade took place this morning. I wrote home in the afternoon. The weather is keeping up well.

The front was never far away, the endless tattoo of the guns rumbling like a requiem:

Saturday 18 August 1917: The usual routine was carried out today.

Sunday 19 August 1917: I was at church service this morning and I enjoyed it.

Monday 20 August 1917: The programme was as usual today.

Tuesday 21 August 1917: This evening we were paid out. We expect to shift tomorrow up the line.

Wednesday 22 August 1917: We are now settled in dugouts in a forward area awaiting further orders. The weather is grand [Kemmel].

Thursday 23 August 1917: I slept well last night. This front is far quieter than the one we've come from. I am awaiting a parcel from home.

Friday 24 August 1917: I was on fatigues last night so we didn't reach camp till about 3.15 a.m. this morning. After a drop of fancy tea I retired and slept till breakfast at 8 a.m. After breakfast I again retired until 11 a.m. then went to the baths. My long lost parcel arrived this afternoon. It was a good one, above all expectations. I don't think there is a fatigue party tonight.

Saturday 25 August 1917: Alas we had to turn out last night. I wrote home today.

For Tommy, as we've seen, war was a mix of utter tedium, backbreaking, numbing fatigue, discomfort and continual grousing – the soldier's timeless lot. From time to time, this disagreeable routine would be livened by sudden danger, the slow build-up of tension before a raid or an attack and then the surging adrenalin of action.

Darkness brought no rest in the line. It brought Tommies out like swarms of worker ants to carry up, to build, to repair, to dig and make good. No-man's-land was any man's land after dark, the muffling blanket of night lit as though by shooting stars as the Verey lights went up:

Sunday 26 August 1917: Yet again we were out last night but there wasn't much work done. I wonder if we go out tonight. I received a letter from home this afternoon.

Monday 27 August 1917: We got a rest last night and we were lucky as the weather suddenly broke down. It rained heavens hard. The poor fellows who had to go came back soaked to the skin. This morning they were drying their clothes in the sun. I suppose I'll be on tonight and it still looks like being stormy.

Tuesday 28 August 1917: The weather was too stormy last night much to everyone's joy as it prevented us from going to work. We were paraded today to hear the sentence of five deserters. One got death [Private Stanley Stewart, 2 RSF executed by firing squad at Kemmel on the 29 August 1917] and four got 15 years. We go to work tonight. The weather looks doubtful.

Shot at dawn remains one of the enduring controversies of the war. The accused was tried at battalion level then the sentence handed up to brigade, then division, to corps and army and finally to the commander-in-chief. Haig commuted some 90 per cent of the death sentences:

Wednesday 29 August 1917: We arrived as usual this morning at 3 a.m. I slept in for breakfast. The weather looks as if it has set in for the winter. We shift up the line tonight [Neuve-Église].

Thursday 30 August 1917: We arrived all right last night at the reserves. I wrote home last night before leaving. The weather is still dull.

Friday 31 August 1917: We have to stay in our dug outs during the day as we are under observation. There is nothing to do here but listen to shell fire.

Saturday 1 September 1917: We have to keep under cover here. Work for us tonight.

Arthur was never more right than when he wrote that line:

If ever I have cause to remember a date, that date is the 1st September 1917. The following incident accounts for my long memory. That day, as usual certain platoons, including my platoon, had been told off for a working party that night. The orders were simple enough. We were to proceed to a certain spot, where an R.E. officer would await us, and give us further instructions.

As soon as the job was done, we would march back and that would be our turn by, for a night or two. At this time, we were occupying, as the diary states, the cushiest trenches it has ever been my lot to live in. The sketch of 'The Reserves' near Neuve Église, I think, carries out to the full, the impression I had of them. They were situated about 3km to the south of Neuve Église. The 'fall in' was to take place after dark, so, as we had an hour or so to spare, my pals and I, had a drum up, and prepared our dugout so as to enable us to turn in, immediately on our return.

Whilst supping my tea, a strange sense of foreboding suddenly swept over me; for an explanation of this, I'm entirely at a loss, but never before, or since, that is to the time of writing this, did a conviction of coming disaster strike me so strongly. However a soldier's feelings are never allowed to interfere with duty – that is, his mental feelings – so I had to make the best of mine, and chance it. The memory of that night vividly remains with me in all its detail.

As the party 'fell in' on the parapet, the full moon was suspended like an enormous arc lamp, from, a vast blue black space, studded here and there, with diamond like stars. Not a breath of wind stirred the atmosphere, but never the less, the night was balmy, in fact it brought to mind the many different scenes that take place under the same moon. Whilst I was standing there at that moment, full of apprehensions, and in the shadow of ruthless war, miles away, and under the same moon, but amidst more appropriate surroundings, lovers would be exchanging sweet nothings, according to their kind.

Dear reader, I'm becoming sentimental, so I'll get on with the war. Having called the roll, we moved off across the field, through which the trenches ran, and struck the light railway, up which we travelled. Little did some of the poor lads know that this was their last march.

We were travelling light, only having skeleton equipment, box helmet, and rifle, and bayonet, so our walk was fairly comfortable. Bye and bye, we came to a place where a road cut the track, and just here stood a truck. Providence was kind in placing it there, as will be seen as the story proceeds. The party turned into the road, and formed up, two deep, at the side. The R.E. officer was conspicuous by his absence, so before our own officer started in search of him, he, being a decent sort, gave the order 'fall out' on the side of the road, but don't smoke. Some sat on the bank, some squatted in the ditch, and there were two, one on each side of the road, while others collected in small groups.

Now as this road ran towards the front line, Jerry had it well taped, and casualties were many hereabouts, so it had been decided, that a communication trench should be made for use, instead of the road. That was to be our job. When the order was given to 'fall out', being in a moody frame of mind, I stood where I had halted. I did not feel inclined to talk, so remained leaning on my bundock, gazing at the moon, and ruminating on what vastly different scenes it was witnessing. The night was still, and for a wonder, the artillery were having a night off. Only an infrequent clack of a rifle, or still more infrequent stutter of a machine-gun, indicated the war was still on.

Around me, the murmur of hushed voices, and an occasional quiet laugh, mixed with the musical jingle of equipment buckles, and rifle swivels, and toned down by the scraping of boots, and rifle butts, on the hard earth, seemed to harmonise with the sense of feeling that goes with a vast open space. But like a menacing, no, more than that, oh how shall I describe it? I can't, I can't, but I felt that the angel of death, hovered over us that night, and the moon seemed to sympathise with us, in an inscrutable sort of way. How long we waited I know not, but I was gently pulled back to earth, by the quietly spoken command of the officer to 'fall in'.

That quiet order was like the crack of doom Oh God! My presentiments were coming true, too true. No sooner had we formed up, than Boom! Bang! Crash! Crash! Whiz! Boom, a German battery was registering on the road, with every shot. Verily the friends of Hell let loose in the form of 5-9 shells. At the outset the officer came running down the line shouting 'Steady boys,' he, by the way, was among the first to be hit. We hesitated a few moments, but the deadly precision with which the shells landed, was too much for us.

Now the German artillery had earned my respect from since ever I knew what shell fire was, and I can tell you, that night he doubly earned all the respect that I can render him. His battery opened out on the head of the road and the fire swept down towards us like a hurricane, in fact it was a typhoon of splinters and death.

To run was as bad as to stand. There was nothing but to literally fling ourselves into the ditches. Personally speaking, it was absolutely a miraculous escape for me, as the diary shows, for so sudden and swift was the fire that the head of the column was nothing short of a mangled, riven state of humanity and the fringe of the death dealing zone, had already travelled my length, before I was in one of the ditches.

What a night! How could I ever possibly forget it? As I took an occasional peep over the top of the ditch, I could see the road clearly in the bright moonlight. Ah! What a change in a few moments, no sounds of quiet laughter or musical jingles now. No moon gazing or ruminating. No! No! That sentimental moment was past. This is war; grim, death-stalking havoc. I saw the peaceful road of a few moments ago. Oh my God what a sight. Bodies lay dotted along it. Big shell holes gaped here and there but, worse than all, the moans, and shrieks, of the unfortunate men. By this time, the fire had slackened, and was not so greatly concentrated on the road.

I do not soften these pen pictures, dear reader, because, only by a detailed account can you possibly half-realise the terrors of such moments. Only your presence at these times could give you full realisation. Some of the bodies lay in that limp, unnatural, distorted attitude that denotes death. Some struggled madly, thoroughly unnerved, but with their wounds, unable to much more than crawl; the others worked their limbs feebly, like sleepy children, while their blood dyed their khaki with big black stains.

Now that the shelling had moved off a bit, the more fortunate of us, pulled our scattered senses together, and climbing from the ditches, helped the wounded to that heaven sent truck. The dead lay in company on that road that night, with the inscrutable moon shining, still as serenely as ever. Whenever the truck was loaded up with our human freight, away we went, hell for leather, each man pushing harder than the next. Although at every bump we heard a groan from somebody, we didn't slacken our pace, and it must be remembered, our nerves were badly frayed, if our skins were whole. If any wounded man went quicker to a dressing post, without taking a motor, I should like to meet him.

For a change of conditions so complete, in such a short period, to my way of thinking, it is absolutely unbeatable. Since that night I am an unconvertible fatalist, and I often think on the verity of the saying 'In the midst of life we are in death'.

Sunday 2 September 1917: What a night last night. We were shelled to blazes. I had a very narrow shave. One fellow in front of me had his head blew off. The chap beside him was severely wounded. The chap next to me was wounded and one of the chaps behind me was killed and the fellow beside him was wounded. I completely escaped. That was everyone round me were either killed or wounded. We lost about a dozen all told. We moved forward this morning [Kemmel].

In 1914, strategic air power was more in the realms of H.G. Wells or Jules Verne. Three years later it was a reality and troops had to add the horrors of regular strafing from the air as well as by artillery to their ever-expanding litany of woes:

Monday 3 September 1917: The aeroplanes were busy last night. Some civilians were killed near us. Nothing fresh happened. I received a letter from home.

Tuesday 4 September 1917: The weather is glorious. We are going up the line again today.

Wednesday 5 September 1917: I wrote home last night. We are settled down for a week's fatigues now. The weather is fair at present. We were paid out today.

Thursday 6 September 1917: Today passed pretty quietly. I hear our boys captured a few lines of trenches this morning.

Friday 7 September 1917: We shifted to another camp today. I hear we shift into the trenches tomorrow.

Saturday 8 September 1917: Our shift is cancelled till tomorrow. Today has been the quietest I have experienced in France for we are quite near the firing line and we have not heard a shot all day. Any other day we are nearly deafened.

Sunday 9 September 1917: We were working from 9 a.m. till about 5 p.m. today. Some Sunday, What!

For Arthur Roberts, bloodied in the Battle of Pilckem Ridge and by now a regular veteran, returning to the dangerous cave like existence of the trenches was all in a day's work:

Monday 10 September 1917: We were working again today. We start for the reserves tonight [Wytschaete].

Tuesday 11 September 1917: We reached our appointed position last night all right. After a lazy day under cover, we go into the front line tonight. I received a parcel.

Wednesday 12 September 1917: Last night we entered the firing line. My platoon is out in front in the shell holes. It is cushy enough.

Thursday 13 September 1917: After another cushy day we were relieved for the front line this evening.

Friday 14 September 1917: We have had a rotten day. Jerry has shelled this line like mad. He brought down one of our aeroplanes but it fell behind our lines. I sent home a P.C. [postcard].

Saturday 15 September 1917: Today was fairly quiet but Jerry usually manages to catch one or two every day with his whizbangs. One of our lance corporals stopped a whiz-bang. He fell on the rations, covering them with blood, so we couldn't eat them.

This must pass for one of the war's pithiest obituaries. Death was by now so constant a companion, the daily attrition of the front line so inevitable, that mere mortality passed into the commonplace:

Sunday 16 September 1917: Jerry strafed us severely early this morning but he cooled off after getting one or two victims. We clear out from this hell tonight.

Monday 17 September 1917: We reached the supports safely last night. It can't be worse than the place we've left anyhow.

Tuesday 18 September 1917: Jerry strafes this place too but it's nothing like the front line. We feel safer here though he lobs over fairly heavy stuff. I wrote home.

Wednesday 19 September 1917: These trenches are cushy; nothing doing.

Thursday 20 September 1917: Business is still slack around this quarter. It suits us fine.

The old sweats had lost any vigour for glory, the old maxim, 'never volunteer for anything' firmly uppermost:

If the diary is opened at 21 September 1917, it will be seen that on that night, I was acting as guide to a ration party. Now if any party, whether ration, working or inspection party, went out, a guide was invariably sent with them.

It saved time and often lives. A man who knew the ground, or said he knew the ground usually secured the job. To be a good guide, a person must have a good sense of direction in big open spaces, and also have a retentive mind for landmarks. I discovered I was in possession of these qualifications to an extraordinary degree. The result was, whenever my company was out I had the guide job.

All parties up the line were without exception, hated by the men, for they were ticklish jobs. I was never partial to them in the least, but as I used to say, that if one must go, then one might as well go as light as possible. For instance, if the turnout was a ration party, then every man had to carry, either a Dixie of tea, or soup, a bag of loaves, a bag of cheese, a bag of jam, a box of biscuits, or a jar of rum, but the guide carried nothing but his rifle, I think my reasoning was sound.

These parties were looked on in a serious light by men engaged, as casualties were very frequent; but like most serious matters of the time, they afford a smile or two later on. Perhaps dear reader, your imagination will enable you to work up a smile, though to us the matter was serious enough at the time.

On this particular evening, my company was lying in the supports, having been relieved from the front line four days previous. The men having been told off for the party, were 'falling in', so being guide, I took my position at the head of the small column, and away we went. All ration parties set out after dark, and hurry to return before dawn, the reason is obvious. Having travelled the road a few times, I knew where all the short cuts and easy stretches were, so we progressed rapidly. Every man had his load, and of course his trusty rifle, and in the darkness their shapes were very grotesque. I always, when I used to look back at the ghostly shadows following me, imagined that I was a leader of a phantom army.

The night was warm and black as pitch, but Jerry's occasional Verey lights kept us in the right direction. Now and then a stray bullet passed near us with its faint Hiss-s' sort of sound. The long range shells were flying over-head, and muffled explosions were faintly heard on the slight wind.

Taking it all round as far as we were concerned, we were having a good enough night. On leaving supports, our way lay along a stretch of well holed road along a very much battered railway, and on reaching a certain point on it, a cut had to be taken across some fields through which the front line ran. Halfway on our stretch of railway, was a German dugout, and about halfway between that, and the front line, laying right across the rails was one of our tanks practically battered to scrap iron. These places were used by runners, or any troops, if caught by shell fire on the railway. This night, however, as I have already said, we made good headway, and in a short time we were tumbling into the front line trenches with the rations in the best of spirits. [See sketch 'Frontline Near Wycheate [*sic*]']

As usual the boys exchanged views of the front line, and supports, and various other topics, while the corporal went in search of the company captain for a receipt. Things were very quiet that night, so the party rested for about twenty minutes. Now the boys never liked Jerry to be too quiet, as they always thought he was planning mischief, so the Dixies, etc., of the previous night were collected and with encouraging advice to me about short cuts, we started back much lighter and quicker than we came.

The fields were soon crossed, and we dropped on to the railway. So far everybody had held together, and we were at once able to proceed which we did at the jildy [quickly]. Down the track we went at a nice four miles an hour pace, which was good considering the equipment, rifle and load that each man had (excluding myself) to say nothing of the numerous shell holes to go round, and twisted rails to look out for. Soon the old tank loomed ahead like a giant with his head between his knees. Like a thunder clap, the Bosche opened out on the front line, and the night was rent with ear splitting detonations. 'We just left the line in time,' says the corporal, as we hastened in good order for the dugout. I spoke too soon, we had advanced about 20yds past the tank when Whiz! Bang! Boom! A battery was switched onto the railway.

Phew! What a show! Big shells, little shells, high explosive shells, and gas shells all burst on or near the track. This was no time to stand about idle. 'Hello there! Skates on for the pillbox,' I cried and valiantly led the boys to safety. Now the majority of the party were old hands and although scurrying for shelter like rabbits, they were thoroughly self possessed. Some of the newer hands became unnerved and they ran, shedding Dixies and Dixie lids or whatever they thought impeded them, always excepting their rifles. One old chap got proper wind up, but he clung on to his Dixie like a hero.

He was roaring like a bull for somebody to help him along, the more he was being left behind, the more he was becoming excited and the more he roared; but the tighter he clung to his Dixie. As I looked back, by the light of the now numerous Verey lights, I could dimly see the old chap struggling along, and nobody near him, and a wave of sympathy swept over me. I waited till he came panting up, then with the Dixie between us, we followed the boys who by this time had made the pillbox in safety.

The fire had increased every moment, so that now a regular barrage was let down on this area. As we lay in the dugout, we could hear great masses of steel rail, and big lumps of shrapnel, and nose-caps, striking the concrete with heavy dull thuds. There is no doubt that that German invention saved some good British lives that night. We were kept here until the fire died down about an hour and a half later. During this interval, the shortage of utensils was noticed.

'Well,' said the corporal, 'unless you chaps want to be charged for these things you'd better go back and look for 'em' – the unfortunates went. When they got outside some forgot whether they had come by the track or the fields, consequently somebody was finding somebody else's lost article but kept it, trusting to be able to change it for the right article on returning to the dugout. That night, I risked getting a thick ear because whilst looking on during the search, I asked if they were looking for souvenirs. At last, however, everybody was complete, and we proceeded on our way, reaching the supports without further interruptions. The scamper for safety and afterwards the hunt for the abandoned utensils is now, for me, a very laughable incident of the past, but at the time, our fate was in the lap of the Gods. In common parlance it was – 'A Narrow Shave'.

'Daddy' Plumer was to focus on the Gheluvelt Plateau. As at Messines, 'bite and hold' was the tactical reality, whereas breakthrough was a headline for politicians. At this stage only the former was viable. Plumer was a great believer in the value of training – 'sweat saves blood':

Friday 21 September 1917: I was guiding a ration party last night. I nearly won a wooden cross on my way back. We shift to another part of the line tonight.

Saturday 22 September 1917: We are in reserves and I am well settled down with my chums. The weather is grand [St-Eloi].

Sunday 23 September 1917: Barring a little light shelling this place is cushy.

Monday 24 September 1917: We were working in no man's land last night. Things are quiet.

Tuesday 25 September 1917: Nothing to report.

Wednesday 26 September 1917: Things are going so well. Perhaps the war is petering out. I don't think.

Thursday 27 September 1917: This is grand. Jerry ignores us and everything in the garden is lovely when he is quiet. I have just started writing and Jerry is searching for our batteries. I hope he keeps quiet while we are shifting out tonight.

Friday 28 September 1917: We marched out last night and not a shell came near us. We are now on our way down the line. This morning I was called before the doctor [Lindenhoek].

Saturday 29 September 1917: We are now in Brigade reserves. Jerry is getting it hot judging by the noise of artillery fire. I've heard no more of this doctor business. I hear a rumour that it is for sending me down the line but it sounds too good to be true.

For Tommy, a proven medical condition or a wound just serious enough to rate a 'blighty', came as a benediction. To be fully fit was far from an aid to survival.

6

THE OLD SWEAT

The Third Battle of Ypres ground on in ghastly, unending attrition. Both sides bled copiously yet the British could not break through the dense belt of fortifications that comprised the Flanders Line. The weather was on Crown Prince Rupprecht's side. For many the glutinous, noxious morass of the battlefield (though in fact there were several) would come to be the defining image of the war. For Arthur Roberts and his comrades, the war descended into a form of limbo, a kind of routine. Out of the line, the war must have seemed like a distant thunder, all was now mundane:

> Sunday 30 September 1917: I was at church this morning and in the afternoon I was put into a hut building detachment. I am now settled in one of the new huts and we are supposed to remain here for ten days.

> Monday 1 October 1917: Reveille was at 6 a.m. this morning, breakfast at 7 a.m. after which work started at 7.45 a.m. till 12.15 p.m. After dinner work recommenced at 1.45 p.m. till 4.15 p.m. I am a painter or supposed to be anyway. I received a letter from home this afternoon.

In moments of great idleness, the army reverts to spit and polish or to painting every surface that can be coated:

Tuesday 2 October 1917: The painters were less busy than yesterday. Some job!

Wednesday 3 October 1917: The painters are stuck for paint so work is suspended meantime. I wrote home yesterday.

Thursday 4 October 1917: The painters have entirely stopped and are sweating on a month's pay.

Friday 5 October 1917: Still no paint; I'm beginning to think we are ornaments though we don't make bad ornaments. We were paid today. I'm going on the spree tomorrow night.

Saturday 6 October 1917: The work is progressing well but the weather has broken again. The rain is on for good I'm thinking so at least I can't go to town tonight.

Sunday 7 October 1917: The weather has entirely broken so the spree is still off. Work was resumed until the rain drove us under cover.

Monday 8 October 1917: Today cleared up a bit, but only till evening when it started to rain as if making up for lost time. However a few fellows and myself resolved to visit the town [Dranouter] even if we had to swim back. Between us we nearly cleared one shop of P.C.s [postcards]. On our road back it was so dark that we only knew if we were together by the glow from our fags. We were drenched on arriving at the camp.

Tuesday 9 October 1917: My leg is beginning its old tricks again so I went to a doctor this morning and got L.D. [Light Duties] I wrote home.

Wednesday 10 October 1917: I attended the doctor again this morning and was excused duty. I am to report sick until Sunday then I attend a board.

'Trench' foot was so-called because the condition arises from prolonged exposure to damp and unsanitary conditions. Flesh becomes discoloured and swells; a pervasive bad odour is an early sign of possible gangrene. If the condition worsens and necrosis sets in, amputation may become the only remedy. With treatment the patient will recover but, like Arthur, may be liable to recurring problems for life:

Thursday 11 October 1917: I was at the doctors again this morning but as our detachment left this afternoon for the Battalion, preparatory to going into the line, I was sent to the 97 F.A. [Field Ambulance] to await the board. [Dranouter]

Friday 12 October 1917: This place is fine. The food is excellent. The beds are grand. I've had the best bath I've had since landing in France. The rain came down in buckets last night and I couldn't help but think of the lads in the line. They must have been up to the waist at least.

In addition to death, wounds and lasting trauma, permanent damage to health was a frequent consequence of trench warfare. Even in the age of industrial warfare, disease could take as heavy a toll as high explosive:

Saturday 13 October 1917: I have lain in bed today thinking of home and several other things. The weather is simply terrible. Winter is in with a vengeance now.

Sunday 14 October 1917: I attended a service this afternoon. A poor fellow who is struck deaf and dumb and has shell shock is now my bed mate. It nearly makes one over emotional to see him. He's practically helpless and at present he is a physical wreck. I appear before the board tomorrow.

Monday 15 October 1917: I was at the board today. It consisted of an officer and two clerks. The officer inspected me and dismissed me with an 'all right'. I shall likely hear the result tomorrow. I did a bit of singing this evening on a small stage accompanied by a piano. I made not a bad show and received lavish applause.

Medical Boards were there to assess a soldier's fitness for duty and to weed out 'shirkers'. They were apt to be unsympathetic. The ethos was about 'making-do'. Duty was the overriding concern. Besides, by this time, reinforcements were in short supply. The terrible attrition in Flanders had emptied Haig's barrel of willing warriors and the new conscripts were regarded as lesser specimens than their volunteer predecessors:

Tuesday 16 October 1917: Today I was returned to my unit but my leg won't last, I'm afraid [Kemmel].

Wednesday 17 October 1917: I was at the doctors this morning but after rubbing my leg with some oil I was dismissed. We leave for the front line tonight. I hear some letters have come for me during my absence but I suppose I'll get them some time.

Thursday 18 October 1917: I saw for the first time a German aeroplane being brought down yesterday. We reached the supports in safety last night. Jerry kept bumping us pretty hard today but during the night he looked as if he meant to wipe us all out [Wytschaete].

Excitement in the skies was not only continuing but increasing as the air war entered a new phase. The age of aces was coming to an end, the short glorious span of a wartime 'celeb'. Larger formations were taking over. Fast, reliable, well-armed scouts or fighters contended the parallel battlefield above the line.

The guns too were becoming even more deadly, sound-ranging and flash-spotting had raised the stakes in counter-battery work. The German artillerist 'Breakthrough' Muller was laying the ground for the devastating offensives to be unleashed in the spring:

Friday 19 October 1917: Our guns seem to have discovered the offending battery for they have been battering Jerry all morning and have received no reply. Jerry replied in style this evening. Not 'arf.

Saturday 20 October 1917: After a quiet day we were relieved this evening. We left the trenches without a shot being fired at us. We have reached the reserves and I am waiting dead tired, cold, and covered in mud for my rum ration.

Sunday 21 October 1917: I am sorry to say that I was drunk last night. I have a hazy idea of feeling queer but that's all. I got a letter from home today [Kemmel].

Arthur's recurring foot problems became a feature of service life:

Monday 22 October 1917: I was at the doctors today and got M & D [Medicine and Duty]. Pay was dished out this afternoon.

Tuesday 23 October 1917: Things went smoothly today. I received a letter from one of the gals.

Wednesday 24 October 1917: Nothing special has happened today. I have volunteered to sing at the battalion concert so I went to a rehearsal this afternoon. On my way back to camp I called in to see the 'Duds' [Royal Horse Artillery concert party]. They were worth the 3*d* I paid to see them. It was like being in a theatre at home.

Thursday 25 October 1917: The day passed uneventfully but in the evening we went on fatigue.

Everyone hated fatigues, the exhausting, numbing and, anywhere near the front, potentially lethal round of chores. Trenches need to be constantly maintained, sandbags, corrugated iron, wire and timber brought up along with ammunition, medical supplies, rations and, inevitably, an abundance of pointless, bureaucratic garnish:

Friday 26 October 1917: Today was very wet. I got my first love letter today but I'm glad to say Mr Cupid missed me. I was at the 'Blue Birds' this evening. On arriving at camp I went for my rum and was informed that I was going down the line tomorrow.

Saturday 27 October 1917: I arose cheery this morning and whilst the boys were preparing for a C.O.'s inspection I was packing up my troubles in my old kit bag [a pun on the popular song]. I paraded at the orderly room at 10 a.m. and received my papers. I had to travel to a certain town and catch the train.

On arriving at this town I was told to appear at the station at
8.15 a.m. tomorrow. Meanwhile I was billeted in a garret with
other lads for the night [Bailleul].

This wasn't a medical discharge but Arthur wouldn't be going
back into the front line, a lot most of his comrades would have
welcomed:

Sunday 28 October 1917: What a night I spent, and what cash
I spent last night. I went to a concert to pass the time and on
returning to billets I immediately got down to it. I couldn't
sleep for cold. About 7 a.m. I went for some coffee then I
started for the train. A big crowd of German prisoners came
on the same train. It was some train. More like a horse bus.
On changing trains I managed to get a first-class carriage. This
train took the usual French time to travel a few miles but after
great sufferance we arrived at our destination safely [Étaples].

By this time, late 1917, after the huge slaughter on the Somme
and at Ypres, few, particularly those in khaki, maintained any illusions. The war had ground on far longer and cost far too many
lives to remain popular:

Monday 29 October 1917: This morning I was put into my
I.B.D. [Infantry Base Depot]. I received a full rig out, a bath
and a small pay. I received also a letter from home and one
from one of the girls. I'm now going to the pictures after
posting some letters home. It's raining cats and dogs.

Tuesday 30 October 1917: Today was also wet. I wrote a few
letters to friends and went to the pictures. This is grand after
being up yonder. I think I am for a medical board. During the
show I met one of the corner boys I knew at home.

Wednesday 31 October 1917: I was in front of the Adjutant this morning and he took down my complaint and effects. I was then put to work in the dining hall. It is fine, plenty to eat and no remarks passed.

Arthur does not comment further or define what he means by 'remarks', whether this tantalising glimpse implies reference to skin colour we cannot say:

There was a Halloween party this evening when the boys ducked apples, scrambled for nuts and apples, ate treacle scones, and played all the children's games. It was comical.

Thursday 1 November 1917: I was at the A.I.D. this afternoon and this evening I was informed that I have permanent base. I hope this is goodbye to the trenches.

Friday 2 November 1917: This morning I was paraded and taken to base details. In the afternoon I was given a job in No 1 Canadian General Hospital. I could stick this for duration.

Saturday 3 November 1917: I was at No. 1 again today. The fags and matches were issued today. This afternoon I sent home the first begging letter since I came to France. I hope I haven't begged in vain.

In Tommy parlance, Arthur had found a 'cushy' billet – every soldier's dream!

Parcels from home were eagerly awaited, hungry for news from the 'real' world back home and those treasured delicacies, supplies of tobacco, that helped make service life that little bit more bearable:

Sunday 4 November 1917: I was lucky to be in a church parade this morning instead of a fatigue party. The service was splendid. I went to town this evening. As I had no money I could not judge the place fairly.

We know Arthur was a churchgoer and that his faith would increase as he matured and, in any circumstance, prayer was preferable to fatigues!

Monday 5 November 1917: Lucky again to be in the party that got excused fatigues this morning. In the afternoon we were told to parade at 5.15 p.m. for night work. When the time came it was found that D. Coy. wasn't needed. I then spent the night watching billiards in the YMCA.

Tuesday 6 November 1917: I was set to work in the dining hut this morning and I left it with nearly half a loaf in my possession. Today has been very wet. I was excused fatigues this afternoon but I have to parade at 5.15 p.m. for night work.

Wednesday 7 November 1917: Today was very wet. As I was out till 11.15 p.m. last night I slept again after first parade till dinner time. I was excused afternoon parade to do more night work but as luck would have it, I was excused that also as I was on last night.

Thursday 8 November 1917: I received my pay this afternoon.

Eureka! Working parties were a constant feature of the hours of darkness, welcomed by none:

Friday 9 November 1917: I was on guard today so I won't be free until tomorrow at 9 a.m.

Saturday 10 November 1917: The guard was relieved this morning so we had the day to ourselves. Fags were dished out after tea. I went to see Lena Ashwell's concert party, it was top hole. [Lena Ashwell (1872–1957) actress and manager, organiser of entertainments for the troops during the Great War]

Sunday 11 November 1917: I went on church parade this morning but as the church hut was full before the whole party got in the surplus was dismissed. I went to the pictures this evening.

In one year's time, on 11 November 1918 at 11 a.m., the war would end and a silence, almost surreal, would descend upon the scarred battlefields, where the thunder and roar of the guns had been near constant for over four years:

Monday 12 November 1917: Today was a grand day only it was pretty cold. I received a letter and P.O. [postal order] this afternoon so I have not begged in vain. I answered the letter immediately. I'm on guard again tomorrow.

Tuesday 13 November 1917: I mounted with the guard this morning.

Wednesday 14 November 1917: The guard dismounted at 9 a.m. this morning. I was free all day. In the evening I went to the pictures.

Thursday 15 November 1917: We were paid out today so in the evening I intended going to the pictures but on my way I called into the Scouts Hut to see a band and I got so interested that I stayed too long.

Friday 16 November 1917: I was at a rough and tumble dance this evening. No ladies were there of course. It was the first dance I've had since I've been in France. I hear that sixty men can obtain tickets at a franc each for a dance on Saturday week. The ladies will be there and so will I.

Saturday 17 November 1917: I'm on guard again. I think they like to see me on guard.

Tommies, like all soldiers through time, tend to think they're the ones singled out by a vengeful fate for more than their fair share of guard detail:

The grub is good and plentiful on this job. I've been commended on my cleanliness and smart appearance by the C.S.M. [Company Sergeant Major] so I think that solves the riddle. We received our fags this evening.

Guard duty was never popular – cold, uncomfortable and utterly dreary. It was so hard for tired young men to stay awake; falling asleep was a very serious business and subject to draconian sanctions. In the line it was perfectly normal to lean on your rifle with bayonet attached, needle sharp point of the 18in blade against the soft underside of the jaw, so if you sagged, however briefly, you were sure of a very sharp awakening!

By now the great battle had spluttered to a close, drowned in the increasing cold and penetrating wetness that lashed the lakes of mud into even greater obstacles. Passchendaele, a smear of brick dust on the ravaged ground, had finally fallen to the Canadians. There was no breakthrough:

Sunday 18 November 1917: The guard was relieved as usual. After a quiet day I went to the pictures.

Movies were new and welcome means of escape. Life behind the lines, while monotonous, was infinitely preferable to life in the line:

Monday 19 November 1917: There were pictures in the YMCA this evening but they were always breaking down so they were a failure.

Tuesday 20 November 1917: I went to the orchestra in the YMCA this evening. Not bad.

Wednesday 21 November 1917: I'm on guard today. I tried to write home this evening but having nothing to say I gave it up.

Thursday 22 November 1917: When the guard dismounted this morning I made a rush for a ticket for the dance. I got one.

Friday 23 November 1917: I went to the pictures this evening. The dance comes off tomorrow. I received a letter from a friend today.

Saturday 24 November 1917: I was on fatigues today. This evening I went to the dance. The W.A.A.C.s [Women's Auxiliary Army Corps], were there and it was a great success. I'm keeping my eyes open for another dance. I was so late in returning to camp that I had to come in by the back way in order to dodge the sentries. I'm watching the new entrance for a future occasion.

Sunday 25 November 1917: I'm on guard once again. The weather is cold but dry.

Monday 26 November 1917: I went to the pictures tonight after an eventful day.

Tuesday 27 November 1917: I asked the doctor for a day's excused duty this morning and it was granted.

As wars go, Arthur's, once through the terrible, fire-swept frenzy of the Pilckem battle, wasn't proving too arduous:

Wednesday 28 November 1917: I returned to duty this morning. To my surprise we were paid this afternoon. A mine has been washed ashore near the camp. There are many and varied opinions as to its nationality.

Thursday 29 November 1917: I mounted with the guard this morning. The weather is dry but cold.

Friday 30 November 1917: After the guard dismounted I was for a board. I don't know the result as yet.

Saturday 1 December 1917: I was on fatigue this morning. This afternoon I was put into the 889 party. What that is I've no idea. I got equipment but no rifle. I gave the pictures a visit tonight.

Sunday 2 December 1917: We paraded for gas helmets this morning but they can't be supplied until tomorrow.

The Germans had first released chlorine gas at the outset of the Second Battle of Ypres in spring 1915. Since then, ratcheting up the horror quotient, both sides had made ample use of chlorine and phosgene:

I received a letter with sixpenny stamps in it today. This morning I dodged church parade and in the evening I went to the pictures.

Monday 3 December 1917: The gas helmets were issued. I have done a lot of walking lately and my leg is quite sore. Again I was at the pictures.

Tuesday 4 December 1917: I went sick this morning and got light duty. This evening whilst wondering how to pass the time, I'm stony broke, the order came to pack up and be ready to move off by 5.30 p.m. We do so at the appointed time. The train moved out at 7.30 p.m. I've no idea where we are bound but at present we're in cattle trucks as usual.

We will not hear Tommy discussing grand strategy or reflecting on the glory of serving king and country. He was kept pretty much in the dark about the first and had rapidly lost enthusiasm for the second. In fact, a behind-the-scenes battle was raging between Haig and his political masters. Lloyd George loathed his commander-in-chief. Both men were equally proud of their differing social antecedents and Haig was never a good communicator. The prime minister wanted rid of the field marshal but lacked sufficient support. Haig was well-connected and had the ear of royalty:

Wednesday 5 December 1917: After a long cold and weary ride we reached our destination [Le Havre] at 4.30 p.m. It took the usual messing around to settle us in our new billets. They are grand. I had a splendid bath tonight and a stove to sit by like we had in Blighty.

Thursday 6 December 1917: After a bad night's sleep from cold and want of blankets I attended the company office. In the afternoon I was installed as an apprentice fitter. This evening it was grand to stop work and go to my hut with a fire blazing and tea waiting on the table. The blankets have not arrived yet but I made sure to be warm tonight. I wrote home this evening.

Friday 7 December 1917: Things were as usual today. This evening I was given a fortnights [*sic*] pay. I attended a concert also. It was good.

Saturday 8 December 1917: Nothing special happened today. I went to a lantern lecture this evening. No work tomorrow.

Sunday 9 December 1917: No work today. I lounged about until evening when I gambled and lost.

Monday 10 December 1917: Work recommenced today. I was warned for guard this evening. At present I'm in the guard room waiting to mount. We dismount at 6 a.m. tomorrow.

Tuesday 11 December 1917: The guard dismounted this morning but I had to go to work all day as usual. During the dismount I pinched a belt from the equipment because it was better than mine. It's about 7 p.m. now but I am going to bed because I am dead beat.

Largely unbeknown to Tommy, the crisis for the BEF was building during that winter. The collapse of Tsarist Russia and the October takeover by the Bolsheviks had ended the Russian effort and paved the way for a humiliating settlement. War in the east was over and Ludendorff finally had a massive army to redeploy westwards:

Wednesday 12 December 1917: Today I received a letter from home so I answered it and wrote another also. Great discussions are in progress tonight about the Christmas celebrations. Some want whiskey after dinner some want rum some want a barrel of beer while others are not particular as long as it's a drink. What will they get? I wonder?

Thursday 13 December 1917: I was bugler this evening. I went to a play in the YMCA hut this evening. It was fine. The Christmas debate is getting hot.

Friday 14 December 1917: I received a letter from one of the girls this evening.

Saturday 15 December 1917: I received a letter from home today. I wrote back for cash. I also sent my first letter since joining up to Dad.

We see from this, Arthur is still in touch, if not regularly, with his father. He tells us nothing of their relationship. As this is his first communication since donning khaki, we may assume the two are not necessarily close:

Sunday 16 December 1917: I was at church this morning. A bath before dinner did me good. I wrote to some of the girls this evening.

Monday 17 December 1917: This evening I received some Christmas cards and I wrote home.

Tuesday 18 December 1917: Nothing worth noting happened today.

Wednesday 19 December 1917: The weather is bitterly cold. Cigarettes were issued today.

Thursday 20 December 1917: A parcel arrived for me today. The Christmas concerts have started this evening. There were some Americans entertaining us tonight. They were not bad.

Despite this relatively easy life, the front was never far away and the BEF could not rest. November had seen a fresh offensive at Cambrai, where early successes, in part the result of mass deployment of improved British tanks, had soon paled in the face of a sharp German counter-thrust. This battle, which had seemed to promise so much, ended, yet again, in stalemate. Arthur, meanwhile, was flexing his musical talent:

Friday 21 December 1917: I received another parcel and was paid out also this evening. As the bugler is on leave I have taken over the job. Some bugler! What!

Saturday 22 December 1917: This morning the orderly man wakened me late so I rushed out half asleep and half dressed sounded Officers' Mess [usually sounded at 7.30 p.m. as the Officers' dinner call] instead of reveille. I went sick during the day. In the afternoon I got the sack so now there is no bugler. The YMCA gave a free tea to our company this evening.

Sunday 23 December 1917: The boys are laughing yet about my rousing them up with Officers' Mess. I visited a Christmas lantern lecture this evening.

Monday 24 December 1917: Through being too occupied in decorating the hut this evening I was too late to volunteer for church tomorrow.

Christmas day, Tuesday 25 December 1917: Christmas comes but once a year. I rose this morning and had a tot of rum as a livener. Work started half an hour later this morning. We stopped at 12.30 p.m. for the following dinner: Roast beef, mashed potatoes and cabbage, plum pudding and mince pies, figs, nuts, apples and beer. There was a concert in the afternoon. After tea there were pictures followed by a sing song and dance until lights out.

Christmas was the time when the normal hierarchy was reversed and officers served their men at table, a very 'Tommy' custom:

Boxing Day, Wednesday 26 December 1917: We were working today. In the evening there was a concert. As the party was late in arriving roll call was put back half an hour.

Thursday 27 December 1917: It was snowing a little today.

Friday 28 December 1917: We were disappointed this evening. No pay.

Saturday 29 December 1917: I reported at the Company Office this morning for a board. In the evening I went to a concert – one of Lena Ashwell's. It was A1. I intend going to town tomorrow.

Sunday 30 December 1917: This morning I went to church. After dinner I proceeded to town. I was shown the places of interest by one of the boys I met. I am off down again next Sunday hail, rain, snow or thunder bolts.

Monday 31 December 1917: I wrote home yesterday. Today I received a letter from one of the girls and one from home.

This is the last day of 1917. I hope next year will see peace. I am sitting by myself at a big stove fire in a dark hut waiting for the New Year. The hooters are going! Hurrah it's 1918 coming in. I feel sure the last year of war has started. I'll go to bed now.

Arthur was right, 1918 would be the final year of the war but it would be the most testing for the BEF. War in 1918 would rage on a scale never before seen. For a while defeat would seem imminent but then the slow, costly path to final victory begun. Haig, unlike the Whitehall doubters, maintained his almost mystical belief that the Great War would be decided on the Western Front. He would be proved entirely correct.

7

THE NATIVE

Ludendorff's massive counter-strokes, unleashed in the spring, would catch the BEF at its weakest. New infiltration tactics involving highly trained specialist assault infantry, or 'storm-troopers', would deliver a series of debilitating blows. They struck at a time when the line was under-manned and, in places, extremely weak. Like their opponents, the British were also redefining their ideas on fortification but, disobligingly, Ludendorff attacked before these were complete. For Germany, time was running out. Despite victory in the east, the arrival of US forces in the west could still spell disaster:

Tuesday 1 January 1918: It seemed rotten to work on New Year's Day but I had to go. I went to a concert this evening. It was rather too sentimental.

Wednesday 2 January 1918: Today passed very quiet. There was absolutely nothing doing.

Thursday 3 January 1918: I visited a play at the YMCA this evening. I have to appear before the O.C. in the morning on a charge of wilfully destroying a pair of boots. I can safely swear

I have done nothing of the sort. Whether the O.C. will think so or not I am anxious to know.

Military justice was often arbitrary and not infrequently harsh. Destruction of the king's property notwithstanding, the fact that vast quantities of materiel were being consumed daily was considered a serious matter:

> Friday 4 January 1918: This has been an exceptionally eventful day for me. This morning I went to the company office to see the O.C. I was told to report at 1 p.m., and with my escort, for I was under arrest, marched into the O.C.'s office. He listened to the evidence against me but refused to see my witnesses. He then asked me if I would accept his punishment. I instantly refused it. He then gave me the option of his punishment or a court martial. I chose the court martial.
>
> With a few remarks on the seriousness of the case and the choice of court martial in spite of the evidence against me I was marched off to the guard room to await my trial. During my confinement I worked out my defence. About 4.45 p.m. the police came to escort me to the office again. The O.C. now told me there was not enough evidence to convict me and that I had escaped his punishment by a bold stroke. My sheet is still clean but it was a close shave. I am naturally very elated by my success because the corporal who charged me is not a popular man. I surprised more than him on the quiet. I was paid this evening.

It does seem bizarre that with the greatest war in history raging around, regimental 'bull' could remain so punctilious and pervasive. A victory over the petty authoritarian ways of the army, however trifling, became a cause for celebration:

Saturday 5 January 1918: I am fairly in the lime light over this case. All the boys are congratulating me. I've proved my mettle this time and no mistake. The corporal is wild and will try and catch me if possible but I'm wide awake. Trust me.

Sunday 6 January 1918: After kit inspection I went on parade. I loitered about after parade until dinner. I did a little job for the bugler just to let him get out. After tea I went to town. I have experienced a real gay dog's life tonight. France is all right I say war or no war.

For a spirited young man like Arthur, war service, when not in the line, had its compensations:

Monday 7 January 1918: Work was resumed today. No after effects felt from yesterday's sport.

Tuesday 8 January 1918: I went to a concert this evening after a quiet day.

Wednesday 9 January 1918: We were cleaning up for kit inspection tomorrow after another quiet day. Cigarettes were issued today.

Thursday 10 January 1918: I received a letter from one of the girls today. [Arthur remains wonderfully discreet about the 'girls'. He gives us references but never any names, nor details of their letters.]

Friday 11 January 1918: What's wrong? No pay today.

Saturday 12 January 1918: No work tomorrow. Thank God.

Sunday 13 January 1918: Nothing doing, I am broke [Tommy's universal lamentation].

Monday 14 January 1918: Still again that joke.

Tuesday 15 January 1918: Work! Work! Work!

Wednesday 16 January 1918: Ditto! ditto! ditto!

Thursday 17 January 1918: Thank the Lord tomorrow's pay-day.

Friday 18 January 1918: We were paid today.

Saturday 19 January 1918: I wrote home this evening.

Sunday 20 January 1918: I went to town today and spent my pay. The fun is good while it lasts but it does not last long. Still once a fortnight is little enough.

Monday 21 January 1918: Work again today.

Tuesday 22 January 1918: Today I was sent to the officer of works. He gave me a note to give to the O.C. I delivered it. Consequently I got another job. I start tomorrow.

Wednesday 23 January 1918: I started my new job this morning. It is all right. I get a longer lie in the mornings and I'm finished earlier in the afternoons.

The war ground on, Germany was gathering her resources for one last grand offensive – make or break. Lloyd George was doing his best to assist – denying Haig reinforcements:

Thursday 24 January 1918: The job is going well. I think I am being badly neglected. I've received no letter since 31 December 1917. I'm beginning to get uneasy.

Friday 25 January 1918: The day was fine and the job's A1.

Saturday 26 January 1918: I was at a sketch this evening in the YMCA. It was good.

Sunday 27 January 1918: I did a little work this morning and obliged the bugler in the afternoon. I posted another letter home also.

Monday 28 January 1918: I'm waiting patiently for a letter from home.

Tuesday 29 January 1918: I went to a concert this evening.

Wednesday 30 January 1918: Nothing doing and no letter!

With the ghastly butcher's bill continuing to rise through the grim arithmetic of daily attrition, the prime minister and the 'easterners' who favoured indirect action were still a potent menace to Haig and the 'westerners' who saw only France and Belgium:

Thursday 31 January 1918: I went to a concert this evening.

Friday 1 February 1918: I was surprised at receiving a letter this afternoon. I quite thought I had been forgotten. I wrote back home this evening. During the week I applied for 30 francs and got them today.

Saturday 2 February 1918: I visited Lena Ashwell's concert party this evening.

Haig had lost his ally Robertson as Chief of the Imperial General Staff ('CIGS'). He was replaced by the Francophile Sir Henry Wilson, who was all things to all men and a staunch ally of none.

Sunday 3 February 1918: I went to town today and had my photos taken after which I called round to my favourite *estaminet*.

Monday 4 February 1918: Nothing doing, the weather has somewhat broken today.

Tuesday 5 February 1918: I was at a cosmopolitan concert party this evening. It was very good indeed.

Wednesday 6 February 1918: There is a great rumour about a coming air raid, the nights are certainly suitable for one.

Thursday 7 February 1918: So far the air raids are off. I hear I am to get another job tomorrow.

By now the menacing silvered cigars of Zeppelins were history and four-engine Gotha bombers were beginning to give teeth to the concept of strategic bombing. Arthur had more immediate and personal concerns:

Friday 8 February 1918: My new job's rotten. There is too much standing about for me. If my feet are not better in the morning I am going sick. I was at the pictures this evening.

Saturday 9 February 1918: I saw the doctor this morning but he wants me to carry on a while longer. Of course if I get worse I am off to him again. I visited a play this evening.

Sunday 10 February 1918: This morning I went to church. I obliged the bugler this afternoon.

Monday 11 February 1918: Nothing doing at all today!

Tuesday 12 February 1918: I received a registered letter today and it contained a 2/- Postal Order. I replied at once.

Wednesday 13 February 1918: Today is the first anniversary of my joining the army. It is as I've said my first, but I sincerely hope it is my last. I gave my Postal Order to the post-corporal to cash. I'll call for it tomorrow.

Arthur had served for a year. Many, very many, didn't last that long – the average life expectancy of a subaltern (2nd lieutenant) at the front was six weeks:

Thursday 14 February 1918: I received 2-70 for my P.O. This evening I was put into a different hut and I also got my old job back.

Friday 15 February 1918: The job is going fine. After pay this evening I went to the pictures.

Saturday 16 February 1918: The weather is fine but very cold. I was at a concert this evening. It was splendid. I wrote to a lady friend this evening.

Arthur, discreet as ever, does not mention the lady by name:

Sunday 17 February 1918: I forgot to enter that I put in for leave yesterday. I went to town today and got my photos. They are all right. I sent a couple home.

Monday 18 February 1918: The day passed very quietly.

Tuesday 19 February 1918: I received a letter from home today. As I am now sweating on leave I am frightened to do anything in case I'm shoved in the mush and my leave cancelled.

Wednesday 20 February 1918: There was absolutely nothing doing today.

Thursday 21 February 1918: This morning I was working away as usual when all of a sudden on turning a corner I ran into the pay sergeant. 'The very man I have been looking for,' says he. 'Go and prepare for leave.' I nearly took a fit as I was not expecting it for another month at least. However I immediately began to prepare. At 2 p.m. I was paid 100 Francs (£3-13-4) at 3 p.m., the leave party fell in and marched away. I am on the boat now listening to the fellows asking one another where they have come from and where they are bound for and relating their past experiences. I am quite happy. The boat [SS *King Edward*] starts sometime tonight. Nobody knows when.

Friday 22 February 1918: The boat started about 11.30 p.m. last night. What a night. There was a high sea running and the boat I believe was behaving at its worst. Within an hour every body around me was rolling all ways with sea sickness. I nearly killed myself vomiting. Oh what a night. We were seventeen hours on board. Whilst disembarking, I noticed that several sails were twisted and the bridge looked pretty groggy while lots of ports were smashed in. I have just got my seat in the train for London. I'm starving!

We reached London at 12.20 noon. After having a free cup of tea and two sandwiches I went to change my money. Whilst waiting a guide suspecting I didn't know my way about put me in front of the waiting queue so that I got my money changed quicker. He then gave me instructions how to get to Euston to catch the 1.15 p.m. Glasgow Express. With good luck I caught all lift and tube connections and arrived at Euston Station at 1.14 p.m. The train was moving before I closed the carriage door behind me. I have just had a wash and brush up and am now engaged on entering up the day's events as far as I have got. I am anxious to send a wire home. I might manage at Crewe. The train has just left Rugby so I hopped off there and despatched my wire. Now I'm rolling homewards tired but contented.

Wednesday March 6 1918: I reached home about 12 p.m. on the night of the 22 February. I have been very busy since; too busy in fact to enter up the diary day by day. I have enjoyed myself immensely. I catch the 9.45 p.m. train to London. It has been good to be home once more but all things have an ending. However with my luck holding out I expect to be back again in the near future with the same health and strength as I shall leave tomorrow evening, God permitting.

If there is a more exquisite sensation than that of realising a longing for home it is the anticipation of the arrival there while actually on the way, but if there is a greater impatience in shortening the distance between the wanderers and the home I have yet to hear of it.

Home! To one who has never travelled far from it, it is only a name but to one who has been forced to live in a strange land among strange people with strange customs and more over enduring dangers and hardships it is a place of peace and contentment to which other places of welcome are but poor substitutes.

When I saw again the shores of Old England from the deck of the troop-ships bringing me on my first leave from France my joy knew no bounds. When I stepped ashore I felt as if I should like to dance and jump myself tired. Not much time was allowed however for such demonstrations for everything was hustle and bustle and banging and slamming and hauling and jerking in securing seats in the London train.

At London the same excitement prevailed in rushing hither and thither changing money and trains. I shall never forget the stew I got into whilst coming on my first leave. The Diary gives a good description of how I hustled. After I had sent my wire ahead of me all my worries were over and as I sat back in the compartment, the lines of Sir W. Scott seemed very appropriate in my mind to travellers of experience no matter how little the experience:

Breathes there the man
With soul so dear
Who never to himself
Hath said
This is my own my native
Land
Whose heart hath never
Within him burned
As home his footsteps
He hath turned
From wandering on a
Foreign strand

For my part the train could not travel fast enough in fact I wished heartily that I had been acquainted with the Genie of the magic carpet. At nearly every big station free tea was served out. It is a good sight to witness a leave train rolling into a station with every window crammed with cheery faces emitting snatches of popular choruses and uproarious laughter and banter. Yes it is good to see but it is far better to be an actor in the scene. When these trains pull into a station the activity of that station is immediately pushed into top speed. Everybody from station master to chocolate boy speeds up in order to supply as many of the clamorous Tommies' wants as possible before the limited departing time.

In the steamy tearooms the monstrous tea urns empty themselves like magic. The mountains of buns and sandwiches dwindle away to crumbs. Outside on the platform girls trundle wheeled trays along the train calling for empty cups. In some cases the request is granted, in others it is not. The rush continues right up until the whistle blows when if anything it accelerates. Now our trains like time and tide wait for no man, exceptional cases excluded, so that while moving out stragglers take the same liberty as in France and jump on where they think fit. Most of the troop trains were corridors so that it was not necessary to board by any particular coach.

At every stop the programme was much the same. As the various parties left the train at their convenient stations they were given parting cheers from their travelling acquaintances and words of advice and admonitions from the ubiquitous wits such as 'see and don't get run over while your home' or 'don't forget when your times up'. There is an end to the longest journey so after ten-and-a-half-hours' train ride we arrived at the Glasgow Central. Tired and stiff but merry with pleasant anticipations, we gathered together our belongings and put on our boots, for they had been removed for comfort, and put ourselves in order for the very last lap of our different journeys home.

Like a lot of big schoolboys we jostled and pushed our way through the wicket and spread all over the big station, each making for the handiest exit. Everybody seemed to be over-flowing with the milk of human kindness as parting sallies were exchanged. At the exit I chose, I left the last of the boys and started for home alone. I was so pleased to be treading the familiar streets once more that if I didn't actually strut along Argyle Street like a turkey-cock it wasn't because I didn't feel like it.

When I clumped into the house with my heavy military boots and my equipment jingling merrily, I was received with open arms and great manifestations of joy, but like all true heroes I had to appear as if I were only returning from an ordinary continental tour.

Naturally explanations and excuses were exchanged over the tea-cups as regards the non receipts of this and that and the cause of certain gaps in the regular correspondence, my opinion also was called for of the war, rumours then in cir-culation and my denial or verification of the wiping out of this regiment or the cutting up of that regiment was anxiously solicited. Strange to say everything I said was taken as true reports and as I could only talk of my own little bit of the front my listeners as a rule judged the whole front by it, which was ridiculous because the enemy put various pressures on differ-ent sectors when it suited him and vice versa with the Allies, so that the state of affairs were constantly at variance until of course the Allied armies operated under a supreme command.

I know that during my leave I learned more of the progress of the war from the books, and papers than ever I got to know while actually on the scene of operations. This fact seemed to give some difficulty in digestion and so numerous were the questions asked of me and such was the vast amount of knowledge required to answer them that if they were printed and set before all the field marshals who took part in the struggle I'm afraid the nation or some millionaire would have to build an institution for field marshals suffering from insanity caused by severe commotion of the brains.

However, with visions of a soft bed and promises of further information before the leave expired, I was allowed to retire and a movement was never more quickly and precisely carried out. If a good bed was ever appreciated the one I slept in was doubly so that night for I was tired out. The first few days were spent in putting myself on view to my friends. In some cases, quite a novel sensation it was thought that I was lying with mother earth wrapped in an army blanket. In other cases I was, by rumours of course, wounded. The only reason for such ideas that I can think of is that for some time before the Third Battle of Ypres no letter of mine was received at home.

I remember I had written all right but through neglect or otherwise I missed the post-corporal so that I had to keep what I had written, hence most of my friends being in touch with each other and none receiving any letters some of them must have had a bad attack of pessimism and accepted as the cause, the conclusion of the earthly existence of yours truly. Of course I'm only surmising this so I think I can also surmise that when correspondence did reach any of them those who had been informed of my decease had not been informed that I was still to the fore.

At two or three houses, parties were hastily organised for my benefit, money being plentiful in those days. I now settled down to one continual round of amusements, in fact I fairly wallowed in them. Dances, pictures, parties, theatres and everything congenial to a young man of such tastes and in a mood to partake of them, I spent my afternoons in bed and my nights and mornings pursuing my round of pleasure. Yes! Like a man who is dying in a desert for want of water, gluts himself if he is lucky enough to find an oasis so did I fill myself with the pleasures offered me.

The long dreary marches and weary hours spent on the fire-step, the nerve-racking night patrols and the ceaseless activity which is the lot of a soldier under arms were forgotten. Truly I lived up to the biblical phrase 'Eat drink and be merry for tomorrow we die.' When the pleasure sprite takes charge of our time it passes swiftly. My time was indeed well taken charge of consequently it seemed to show its best speed. The evening at last came that found me slowly sauntering toward the station in the midst of many friends each carrying some part of my equipment or one of many send-off parcels.

During a lull in the rather forced cheerfulness I recollected how differently I had moved along this thoroughfare only twelve short nights before. However duty called again and with so many friends around me it behoved me to appear as unconcerned as possible. The railway stations during the war were about the only public places where personal emotions were allowed free rein and were not vulgarly criticised. Many were the scenes of unbounded joy and unfathomable despair witnessed, by the employees and frequenters of these depots. More pitiful was it to see heart breaking feelings miserably hidden under a cloak of pride or seeming cheerfulness.

I recognised several of the chaps whom I came home with amid their particular friends. I think now I have brought you dear reader back to the departure platform. I'll wind up the yarn because I intended this to be a happy experience and besides you may be well enough acquainted with the last moments before a loved one's farewell without me reminding you further. Suffice it to say that I had a jolly good time and was returning to France with a good heart. Anyhow I don't think much of anybody who drinks to the dregs from the cup of pleasure and makes a song about a spoonful of less sweet ingredients!

'Wrote home today' – how frustrating! For Arthur never tells us where home was. He was writing five years after the war and without the need to fear the censor's pen, yet he is still reluctant to name a loved one or give an address. Where was the house he 'clumped into with his heavy military boots', and who 'received him with open arms and manifestations of joy'? The only time in all his writings Arthur mentions a name and an address is his very first entry in the diary: 'If found please send this book to – Mrs Armstrong, 635 Argyle St, Anderston, Glasgow. Finder will be rewarded if his address is forwarded with the book.' From this it can be taken that Arthur knew Mrs Armstrong very well and had made financial provisions with her. In the letter to his aunt, from Duddingston camp near Edinburgh in March 1917, he writes: 'I hope you are drawing the half pay alright.' Could Mrs Armstrong be Arthur's aunt?

So much of Arthur's life has to be inferred, including family relationships and history. For example, he refers to his father in the same letter as 'the Old Boy', a term of familiarity often used between members of the same family, suggesting father and aunt were brother and sister. David Roberts was born in 1865, which gives us a rough age range for his sister. We can also glean from the letter that both Arthur and his father are, at this time, in regular touch with the aunt. Where his father and aunt were born and where his aunt married are unknown.

Electoral rolls, census information and valuation rolls give us some clues to family arrangements and location. Take, for example, the information we can glean about Andrew Alexander Armstrong, who arrived in Glasgow in November 1912, shipping in from Detroit. He is recorded as the head of a family living at 635 Argyle Street from 1913–17, earning a living as a cook. He was born in 1886 and was unmarried when he enlisted in the Canadian Cameron Highlanders in 1916. Could this be another nephew of Mrs Lillah Armstrong?

Private Andrew Alexander Armstrong of the 44th Battalion, Canadian Infantry (New Brunswick Regiment) was killed in action on 23 August 1917. He is buried in Vermelles, a British Cemetery in France. He is also commemorated on a family gravestone in Overleigh Cemetery, Chester. His age is given as 32 and his next of kin are given as Andrew William Armstrong and his wife Frances of 22 Liverpool Road, Chester. A search of the records revealed that the latter's older brother John emigrated to Canada in the late 1870s, where he was joined by Andrew A. Armstrong in 1911. John Armstrong is the right age to be Lillah's husband and this would explain the Canadian connection. The Glasgow Valuation and Electoral Rolls show Mrs Lillah Armstrong living in the same single roomed house at 635 Argyle Street from 1918 until she disappears in 1927.

On the voters roll recorded on 1 October 1918 Arthur is recorded staying at 635 Argyle Street but not necessarily in the same house as Lillah. This was a tenement property and Arthur was probably on leave. If the scenario is correct and the aunt and Mrs Armstrong are one, then Lillah has stayed somewhere in Anderston from the time Arthur came to Glasgow. When she moved into 635 Argyle Street is not recorded, but could have been as early as 1912.

In Arthur's letter to his aunt he implies she has a daughter (Lily). The existence of a female cousin close to Arthur's age might explain why the young boy was living in a lodging house while still in apparent contact with his family. The small restricted tenement spaces would have necessitated the two sharing a bedroom – clearly not acceptable.

The 1911 census tells us Arthur (aged 14) shared a room with four men in the Exhibition Hotel at 38 Clyde Street, Anderston. This room was divided into five self-contained units, each 6ft 2in long by 5ft wide and 7ft high. Each unit was covered over with strong wire mesh netting and contained a bed, locker, wash basin, towels and a spring lock door for security.

This was not an unusual situation – the small size of Glasgow homes had created a demand for such accommodation. Clyde Street may sound like a prison to us but it was regarded as a model lodging house in its time. Arthur remained there from as early as 1909 to at least 1915 – in all likelihood until he enlisted in 1917.

On his way to school in the morning Arthur could well have dropped in at Argyle Street for breakfast, returning for his evening meal before later retiring to the hotel. It is more than conceivable Arthur would spend most of his weekends and spare time there and would consider the place his home, rather than the hostel. His letters make it clear he anticipated all the comforts of a normal family life, regularly receiving letters from his relatives. Invariably, after receiving such a missive, he anticipates a parcel, most likely containing the cake mentioned in August 1917, which, he tells us, he 'demolished'. No wonder he anticipated his freedom from the army with such relish:

Private Roberts, hello, report at the company office tomorrow morning after parade! One evening I was lying down reading when a corporal came to my hut and issued the fore-mentioned order. At this time I was attached to the headquarters of the 33rd Motor Transport Company Le Havre. [A stamped passport of this company can be seen in the diary.]

For some time past, rumours had been going around about extensive demobilising that was taking place. Word had also reached the attached men to this M.T. Coy that our company was rapidly dwindling – guess therefore our jubilation. Those who were reporting on the morrow were in the highest heavens of delight and the subjects of envy of the others. At last we were going home, Oh! Roll on the ship that carries us back.

Next morning the lucky ones were paraded and marched off to No. 2 rest camp. There we were put into bow huts until such time as the required draft was complete. Troops were being called in from all quarters and a day or two elapsed before the draft was at full strength.

About three evenings later the order came to parade with full kit after handing in three blankets to the store. By this time it was known that a start was to be made and long before the time the draft was on the parade ground. It was after dark when we lined up but the roll was called and the demobilisation papers given out by lantern light. All being in order we were marched away to our train which as usual consisted of horse boxes.

Now it mattered little to us what we travelled in so long as it carries us towards home. Late that night we pulled out and my last view of Le Havre was a few scattered lights shining through the darkness. The speed of travelling was just similar to that which I described in a previous article.

It was late the next evening when we slowly passed through Boulogne and drew in to a siding a mile or so further on. The weather was very cold and the warmth of the trucks was soon missed. Forming up on a road that ran alongside the railway, the officer in charge gave the command and we moved off each walking as it suited him best.

The night was very dark and an icy wind was blowing but the weather was quite dry. We walked about three miles when we were halted in an open space of some sort. Now, whether the going home emboldened some of the men or whether standing in the icy breeze in a black night irritated them I couldn't say, but never before did I hear officers and non-coms get their characters as I heard that night.

Of course the delinquents were not discovered on such a night and amid so many men. At last, however, we were divided up, put into tents for the night. I found myself in a marquee where I made myself comfortable and slept soundly. Early next morning we were astir, completed our toilet and had breakfast, after which each man was for a medical examination.

Drafts were pouring into this camp very regularly and as a certain amount of accommodation had always to be available the troops staying overnight were got away as soon as possible next day. In the afternoon therefore we were lined up and away we marched again.

Several drafts must have joined us at different stations and at the camp for I'm sure from the head to the tail of the column was fully half a mile. Some were fully armed some were without any arms at all. Some had big loads some had small loads and some had only haversacks. Some walked as if on air, whistling and joking, others plodded as if through a bog sweating and cursing.

I was fully armed and I had a big load. Yes and I plodded as if through a bog sweating and cursing and like a soldier I can open out when things go up my back like that baggage did that day. Yes dear reader, some behaved this way but everybody was happy, as happy as the live long day. As we drew near our new camp, my eyes lit with joy, at least I think they did, for there before me was the familiar wireless station and the railway beside it. Yes and there was that steep street which some old pals, now lying with the heroes back there, and I had struggled up our first day in France. The camp itself was changed for instead of tents there were rows and rows of bow huts but I knew it as St Martin's Camp.

This camp was certainly different and it was even hard for me to recognise the spot where I did my piquet guard on my first arrival in the camp. I remember that guard very well.

I went on from 2.30 p.m. till 5.30 p.m. The afternoon was beautiful and clear, I myself was full of cheerfulness and patriotic enthusiasm. From my high position on the hill I had a capital view of the town of Boulogne and the harbour. As I have said the day was clear and away on the horizon could be seen the chalk cliffs of England.

Many were the thousands who turned their backs to this scene in the execution of their duty that never saw it again. In we marched to the camp where we were cut up into batches and passed through an inspection hut where all live ammunition had to be handed in. Cut into still smaller batches we were installed in huts until our departure. I must say that in this camp the feeding was excellent. I slept well that night. The next day I thought I'd take a last look round the old camp but the biting icy wind considerably curtailed my wanderings.

Whether some of the draft left that night or not I'm not sure but some of us slept there again that night. Next morning after breakfast however we marched out and down the steep street which is far easier than coming up. Right on to the boat we went and within half an hour we set sail. About an hour later we tied up at Dover and the troops were marched right into the station nearby.

Here some tea was given out before the different trains arrived. Certain trains were for different demob centres but all Scots troops had to get their train at London. In due time we arrived in London; of the big draft I reached Boulogne with, there was only about fifty or sixty got to London. At Victoria station we drew some money then being placed under an officer going north we were taken to Kings Cross.

With the usual bustle of getting from the right platform to the wrong one and from that one to the right one we at last boarded our train. The long journey to Edinburgh commenced. Early next morning we arrived in the Scottish capital and changed trains for Kinross, which was our demobilisation centre. Kinross was a very countrified place so when we were conducted straight from the train to the camp we didn't miss much in the way of amusements.

Here we handed in our papers and received certain ones in return. Deficiency in kit was made good but after I had applied for a new cardigan, during the interval of waiting I thought I could spend the time better in the canteen, consequently when the quarter bloke wanted me I was missing so I was a good cardigan the poorer.

About two hours later we were marched back to the train which we climbed into from the permanent way. The draft had arrived in various states of armament but on leaving the only luggage discernible was kit bags and haversacks. A more exuberant crowd would have been hard to find, amid cat-calls and mimicked military commands and sarcastic and abusive farewells the train drew out and we started homewards free and happy men. Queen Street station Glasgow was the destination of most of the crowd and it was mine also. It did not take me long to reach home and when I did I sat down and felt like a chap just released from a long detention, in a strict institution.

On demob, men were allowed to wear the uniform for a month after, during which time they drew a weekly allowance from the nearest Post Office on the production of a form called a ring-paper. I had a good month's sport before settling down to civilian life and in order to make my severance with the army as sudden as my association with it I wore my uniform and underclothes and even my boots up to the very last day of my month.

For the time at least the hard bed-boards with draughty joints were things of the past. The bugle calls would not arouse me from slumbers. The cares of rifle and equipment had ceased, like an irresponsible brother to worry me. Best of all I was now as good as any officer, regimental sergeant major, or in fact any non-com that ever wore the king's uniform.

When I look back in my own case and see what scenes and changes I've witnessed and experienced and consider how I have been spared not only in life but also in limb, I feel that I've a lot to be thankful for and if I have gained but little of the world's goods in the service of my king and country I have at least been made a man, of which, in my opinion, should be the main aim of every youth.

My self-imposed task is now completed and I hope that by my poor efforts as a scribbler, I have conveyed to the reader a slight idea of how much may be concealed behind a simple statement of very few words. In filling this small book I have not allowed myself much space. In fact, were I to write all it is possible for me to remember of my army life, I should need a few more of these books. It will be noticed that all the incidents related (with the exception of the last) took place in the same year. I have several reasons for this:

1) I wish this book and the diary to corroborate each other.

2) The diary was only written for a certain period of a year and was not resumed on my return to France.

3) That although even the diary itself can only be accepted on trust I did not wish to offer further happenings without its support, however weak, if weak it is counted.

We can only speculate about Arthur's duties between his return from leave in March 1918 and his demobilisation on 5 December 1919. He has left us a list of his various functions in his book of reminiscences without giving dates or locations: company-runner, batman, cycle-orderly, motor mechanic, telephone orderly, dispatch-clerk and aircraft gunner.

His photos offer a clue – one picture shows the airfield at Le Havre, taken from the top of the water tower. Other shots taken round the camp and in the interior of a hut suggest he was there for some time. Certainly, one thing we can be sure of – Arthur's foot condition would not make flying impossible. By 1918 aircraft had become more sophisticated and a second seat had been installed for a co-pilot. These co-pilots were often fully trained soldiers whose experience with the handling of weapons suited them for work as aircraft gunners.

Arthur appears to have brought a personal camera with him when he returned from leave – something that had been specifically banned. He used it as a means of social commentary as well as a means of recording his environment and taking pictures of his friends. One particular shot shows a local backyard with a description of the hostile comments made by the residents. Not that Arthur needed pictures to describe his experiences. His words at the front of the diary were prophetic – 'Sufficient unto the day is the evil there of':

> I have endeavoured in this book to state plainly, truthfully and without pride or exaggeration most of the incidents and experiences which took place day by day. My feelings at times were such as I can't describe so I leave them to the reader's best imagination which, unless he has had some, will produce poor results in comparison with those I can't describe.

Arthur Roberts 11/11/17

8

AS GOOD AS ANY MAN

Sometimes I wish I had continued the record, but I can tell you it takes some doing to fiddle about with a diary, sometimes in pouring rain, sometimes on chilly nights after having trudged for miles and miles or after gruelling spells of digging trenches or carrying shells and such like. At these times you feel like flinging yourself down anywhere so long as you can get off your feet. Yet to be sure of your diary it must be entered up at night, else in such exciting times items may be forgotten and unless rubber is procurable the insertion of words in a small book often makes the writing illegible.

Only in about two cases (of practicable impossibility) have I been guilty of entering up a day late. Yes, under certain conditions a diary is a very impatient and exacting taskmaster. Yet what is the use of commencing it, as everything else, if it is not going to be done right? What I am going to say now may sound strange, but if you tell a funny story you at least expect to cause a smile.

Similarly if I expect a sigh for my serious yarns and a smile for, well I won't say funny yarns, but just the other yarns, I can't be blamed can I? If I have succeeded in producing the foresaid sighs and smiles then I know I have succeeded in my object as put forth in the preface. Should the presumption of my lofty hopes be realised in you dear reader, then may I indeed consider myself exceedingly flattered.

Lloyd George's prediction of 'a land fit for heroes' turned out to be one of the twentieth century's most bitter ironies. The land so many thousands returned to, and the era they were entering, would be one blighted by depression, hunger and despair. War broke out almost immediately in Ireland, there was trouble again on the North West Frontier and Bolshevik Russia became the new bogey man. Versailles heaped ignominy and an insurmountable burden of debt on a prostrate Germany. At home, veterans' medals quickly tarnished, and many were sold or pawned to buy food. An understandable pacifist reaction set in.

The First World War had brought an industrial bonanza to the Clyde, to shipbuilders, engineers and manufacturers. Tens of thousands of Scots and Glaswegians were serving, however, and the war had witnessed the emergence of a radical movement called 'Red Clydeside' led by militant trades' unionists. Formerly a safe Liberal bastion, much of the industrial district had switched to Labour by 1922, finding a strong base among Irish Catholic working-class districts. The women of Clydeside were notably active in building neighbourhood solidarity around housing matters. Where Arthur stood in political terms we cannot be sure – he studiously avoids references to partisan politics. In fact he comes across as rather apolitical.

Even if Arthur does not recount instances of racial abuse, the situation in Glasgow was not always tranquil. In late January 1919 a serious disturbance broke out at the Mercantile Marine Offices located in Broomielaw. This fracas was caused by an alleged preference for the employment of whites in the signing up of crew. The disorder started with words and quickly erupted into a fight, fists and sticks flying furiously. The affray lasted over an hour, escalating when knives and guns were produced. There were numerous casualties and three men were taken to hospital with stab wounds to head and back. One was treated for gunshot wounds to the neck. An eye-witness at the dockside who observed the incident described it as being akin to 'a town out west'!

Thirty men, natives of Sierra Leone, were arrested in the Sailors' Home, where a gun and live ammunition were found. It was said by members of the Seafarers' Union that the 'black' men had come from Cardiff to take white men's jobs. Michael Carlin, aged 23, was wounded in the head by a black man in James Watt Lane and a black man was stabbed in the back and legs. A few days later twenty-seven men from Sierra Leone appeared in court, three of whom pleaded guilty to breach of the peace. One of these, Tom Johnson, was said to have shot Duncan Cowan in the neck. Each was fined £3 3s or given twenty-one days in jail. The sentences imply how cheap life had become in the days during and following the Great War. In the months leading up to August 1919 violence broke out in the vicinity of many ports around the British mainland. These violent attacks on minority workers resulted in five fatalities as well as vandalism to property.

Arthur was clearly not involved in any of this localised conflict. Demobilised on 5 December 1919, he had returned to Glasgow to finish his apprenticeship with Harland and Wolff. An indenture from 14 April 1920 confirms an allowance for time served both during and prior to military service. Clearly the work he had done, servicing and repairing heavy tractors while still in khaki, counted towards his apprenticeship.

Arthur saw his war service as the pivotal point in his life that had to be recorded. For him, as for so many others, the army would be a defining experience. Yet he gives no clue as to the aftermath and never speaks of any lingering psychological (or other) effects. As far as we can see he returns, having 'done his bit' and picks up the threads of his life in Civvy Street.

Harland and Wolff had launched itself in Northern Ireland in the 1860s. Ironically, it was an Anglo-German partnership that prospered mightily and stayed at the forefront of marine innovation, building such giants as RMS *Olympic,* RMS *Britannic* and, most famously of course, the *Titanic.* In 1912 the firm expanded into Glasgow, acquiring and developing a series of yards at Govan. The berths produced large numbers of tankers and cargo vessels and continued to expand through acquisition even as late as 1919. Throughout the war-years bonanza, the yards had built cruisers and floating gun batteries or 'monitors'. Despite hard times after 1918, Harland and Wolff remained a major employer.

The electoral roll of 1 October 1918 shows Arthur on leave at 635 Argyle Street, living in a flat rented by a Mrs Armstrong. The building no longer stands but as no fewer than twenty-six other registered voters are shown at the same address we may safely assume the property was a tenement. Arthur did not complete his apprenticeship till 1921 at the age of 24.

At that time he was living at 29 Stobcross Street, Anderston. We have no information as to his time with Harland and Wolff other than that he moved after some years to another firm, Duncan Stewart & Co, whose works were at Summer Street, Bridgeton (in Glasgow's east end). This move was likely prompted by economic necessity as the post-war depression began to bite and order books dried up.

Arthur had rediscovered his love of sketching and also of music, though he finally laid aside his cherished bugle to pick up a banjo. He confesses to being an indifferent worshipper during the war but was nonetheless confirmed in the Church of St John the Evangelist during 1922. The church lay at the junction of Argyle and Houldsworth Streets in Anderston, very much at the apex of the world he knew from before the war, where he'd grown up. We are aware Arthur was a companionable man and the church would have acted as a spur and outlet for a range of social activities, scouts, music and drama.

It was in the course of 1924 (when he returned to live in the Exhibition Hotel in Clyde Street) that Arthur started sending his personalised Christmas cards. Probably just prior to the end of 1930 Arthur befriended Hugh (or Henry) Finnigan and his wife Jessie. They lived at 7 Ancroft Street, Maryhill. This friendship was to prove significant for Jessie, as she was soon to be widowed. Sadly, Mr Finnigan passed away in Belvedere Hospital in 1935. The friendship between Arthur and Jessie blossomed and in the same year they moved across the Clyde to 16 Shearer Street, Tradeston, where they shared a home and Jessie became Mrs Roberts. We can only speculate as to the reason why they did not marry till two decades later. Around this time Arthur is shown in one of his photos playing in a six-piece ensemble with the Glasgow branch of the British Legion Dance Band.

By 1935 Arthur's occupation is given as an electrician, so whether he had retrained with his current employer also remains uncertain. What we do know is that war clouds were once again rolling across Europe, while Britain, certainly the northern half, was still engulfed in severe economic depression.

Britain was two very different countries in the 1930s. Both north and south had been badly affected by the Great Depression with unemployment in the former reaching 13.5 per cent. But the decade had seen a revival of economic prosperity throughout the Home Counties, with new manufacturing such as the electrical industry and a burgeoning motor transport industry. Leafy and pleasant suburbs spread outwards and standards of living soared – electric cookers, washing machines and radios filled kitchens in garden townships. In the north a very different picture emerged. Here, traditional industries such as coal mining, shipbuilding, textiles and engineering were in marked decline; unemployment spread like a contagion. Millions existed in cramped, unsanitary housing on means-tested handouts, eating in communal soup kitchens, with poverty and squalor spreading disease. Scurvy, rickets and tuberculosis were rife.

The 'heroes' of the Western Front were seen begging on street corners and pawning their medals to survive. Now another war was brewing, one that promised even more civilian carnage than the last. Guernica had shown what indiscriminate horrors modern strategic bombing could unleash. The only thing certain about the coming war was that it would be very much worse than the last. Britain had 'won' the First World War but what was the face of victory? A whole generation of young men blighted in what seemed, in retrospect, a quarrel between bickering members of a dysfunctional pan-European royal family.

There was a feeling that the titanic effort expended during the war was somehow a one-off. The scale, suffering and sheer pointlessness of the whole ghastly mess had led to a view, not surprisingly, that such a thing could simply never again occur. It's not surprising that, as the horrific experience of war receded, to be replaced by the onerous problems of peacetime soldiering, the feeling should grow that the unprecedented war effort of 1914–18 had been unique, even an aberration.

No less an authority than the Chief of the Imperial General Staff, Sir George Milne, endorsed this view in 1926 when he described the Great War as 'abnormal'. At present he added, the army could not even mobilise a single corps; it was most unlikely ever again to be required to fight a European war. The phrase 'Never Again' was frequently used about such a nightmarish prospect; politicians implied scornfully that they would not send troops to 'the trenches' and even use of the term 'Expeditionary Force' was deplored in government discussions and official reports.

Life was hard in Scotland during the Depression and after. The Jarrow hunger marches from Tyneside passed into legend as the potent symbol of a north–south divide. In such difficult times,

Sir Oswald Mosley's British Union of Fascists was able to make significant gains in terms of a popular following. Modelled on and extolling the perceived virtues of Mussolini's Italy, membership rose as high as 50,000 and produced an equally aggressive response from leftist groups. There were violent clashes between both factions in the streets of major cities.

We do not even catch a glimpse of Arthur's life at this time or his role in the war effort from 1939. We do know he was plagued by recurring foot problems, a legacy from his days in the trenches. This may have prevented his joining the Home Guard or any other civil defence organisation. Clydeside would suffer badly during the bombing. This was total war, where civilians and key workers were very much in the front line.

Clydebank's production of ships and munitions for the Allied war effort made it a prime target for the predatory attentions of the Luftwaffe. Major objectives included John Brown & Company's shipyard, ROF (Royal Ordnance Factory) Dalmuir and the Singer Corporation factory. As a result of two concentrated air raids on the nights of 13 and 14 March 1941, Clydebank was utterly devastated, sustaining the worst destruction and civilian death toll in the whole of Scotland throughout the entire war.

A total of 439 bombers dropped over 1,000 bombs, high explosives and incendiary. RAF fighters managed to bring down a brace of the raiders but anti-aircraft fire proved largely ineffective. Some 528 people were killed and 617 more were badly injured, hundreds more were wounded by blast and flying debris. Out of approximately 12,000 houses, only seven remained undamaged — with 4,000 completely destroyed and 4,500 severely damaged. Over 35,000 people were rendered homeless. Arthur and Jessie were lucky – they emerged unscathed even though their home in Tradeston was only 5 miles from the centre of the blitz.

Peace in 1945 brought only austerity and rationing, drab people on soot-blackened streets, long shuffling queues everywhere. The huge cultural changes set to develop in the 1960s would have seemed only a distant Shangri-La. Rumours that chocolate was on sale, however fleetingly, produced significant queues outside Lewis's Department store on Argyle Street. Though the war with Germany and Japan had ended in overwhelming Allied victory, the burden of accrued debt was crippling and the grim spectre of a new war, potentially even more terrible, loomed from the east, across the gulf of a Europe more divided than ever. Scotland entered a period of industrial decline, the pace, slow at first, would prove both fundamental and inexorable.

Most Glaswegians would enjoy only a brief annual respite from work, the traditional Glasgow Fair fortnight at the end of July. We know from their extensive photograph albums that Arthur and Jessie holidayed every year in Blackpool, alongside thousands of others, all determined to make the most of two weeks' escape from toil and drudgery. The couple married there on 1 August 1956. Both gave their ages as 59 (a minor vanity on Jessie's part as she was in fact 62).

One who knew Arthur during the post-war years was Jim Wilson, who was apprenticed as an engineering draughtsman with Duncan Stewart & Co in 1949. Arthur was, at that point, a fitter in the heavy fitting shop and the 16-year-old Jim was apprenticed to him. Jim did not know Arthur beforehand but was aware of his established status within the company and the important nature of his work for them:

> From that day onward until I left Duncan Stewarts' he became my mentor and friend and took a great interest in my progress and gave me every encouragement, not only in everyday practical work but also in my attendance at part time studies, which culminated in my obtaining a Higher National Certificate in Mechanical Engineering and later in becoming a member of the Institute of Mechanical Engineers ...

During the time I spent with Arthur, he was extremely patient with me … he was a real gentleman and it was a privilege and pleasure to have known him.

(Taken from an interview with Jim Wilson)

Arthur does not leave us any diary or memoir for this period in his life. The sole record lies in the photographs. As ever, Arthur is dapper and smiling, very much the man about town, age had not diminished his propensity for a theatrical swagger. He is still very much the sociable type, very much part of his surroundings. The images, like a silent memory, give us a glimpse not just of Arthur and Jessie but of what is now a largely vanished world. Blackpool was the holiday metropolis, cut-price package deals to Spain – still under Franco's iron jackboot – did not yet exist. Blackpool had over twenty summer shows at any one time, including such established 'celebs' as George Formby, a young Ken Dodd and even major Hollywood stars like Frank Sinatra.

Rock 'n' roll was on the horizon and Arthur, always an eclectic-minded music lover, bought his and Jessie's Dansette record player. Manufactured by the London company J. & A. Margolin Limited, the Dansette proved enormously popular – over a million were sold during the fifties. Robust and versatile, the machine could play 7-, 10- and 12-inch discs of 33⅓, 45 and 78 rpm. Times were changing, the shroud of post-war austerity was being lifted and people at last had a glimpse of those 'broad sunlit uplands' Churchill had idealised.

Not Jessie. She died aged 63 in Southern General Hospital in Glasgow. Perhaps the reason for their marriage, after twenty years of cohabitation, was an intimation of impending mortality. Arthur, still at 16 Shearer Street, was now left alone. His record collection, lovingly maintained as befits this fastidious man, shows the wide sweep of his tastes: Mario Lanza, Harry Belafonte, Slim Dusty, Connie Francis and Cliff Richard, all the way through to Abba.

He was no longer young, the world was changing. He was a widower, whose formative experience was a war most people preferred to forget about. A dreadful echo of the Clydebank Blitz occurred during the evening of 28 March 1960. Fire broke out in Arbuckle, Smith & Co's bonded warehouse in Cheapside Street, Anderston. Over a million gallons of whisky and 30,000 gallons of rum were stored there. At 7.50 p.m. the whole lot erupted like a demonic volcano, spewing debris, fire and death. Nineteen firefighters were engulfed; it needed 400 of their colleagues to beat back the flames, which smoldered for another full week. The blaze began less than 100yd from Arthur's old lodgings in the Exhibition Hotel and only 300yd across the River Clyde from his home in Shearer Street, Tradeston.

That night, news of the disaster spread quickly over the city and thousands flocked to the Broomilaw to witness the scene. Who knows, could Arthur have been one of the throng, respectfully threading a silent path slowly westward along the waterfront? Perhaps he remained on the south bank of the river, near the ferry steps, paying his own private respects and remembering how similar this scene was to his time at the front, in France and Belgium, all those years ago?

Arthur was not alone for long. During the later months of 1960, he is recorded as sharing the house with Jean McDonald, Jessie's cousin, who had recently retired. We can speculate that Jean and Jessie were some of the 'girls' Arthur refers to in his diary and memoirs.

Despite Jessie's death, Arthur still holidayed in Blackpool, solitary for a while but not lonely, sociable as ever. The fading resort, fast losing out to Benidorm and Marbella, must have held many happy memories. In the 1960s he stayed at a bed and breakfast in the High Street. The son of the house Steve Wallwork remembers him well – strolling round from his boarding house for his nightly dram at the Imperial Bar in Springfield Road.

It takes little to imagine him sauntering along the promenade, lost in his past. The smell of the donkeys and the noise of the bells round their necks as they were led from the beach at the end of the day would bring back happy memories. Pausing at a favourite spot might bring a smile to his face. A trip on an old Glasgow tram would remind him vividly of home: the last tram journey in Glasgow was in 1962 and was his own number 9 from Auchenshuggle. His own retirement was imminent and he left Davy United (successor to Duncan Stewart) in April 1962, though he remained active in its retired employees club, acting as treasurer for a time.

In 1968 – the year of youth protests across Europe, the Prague Spring and the Tet Offensive – Arthur and Jean moved to 112 Craigmuir Road, Penilee. This was probably a forced move as their previous house was caught up in the construction of the new Kingston Bridge. Arthur seems to have remained in touch with family back in the West Indies (where we know his father had returned at some point). On the back of a letter found among his possessions is a sketch plan of the house in Penilee and an address – Clydesdale House, c/o GPO, Scarborough, Tobago, BWI. The letter itself offers no clues – it is from the Davy United Retired Employees Club.

Jean died in 1977 at the age of 82. Arthur, who registered her death, is described as a 'friend' on her death certificate. He moved briefly to 12 Bowfield Avenue, Penilee, while the property was upgraded. In 1979, two years after Jean's death, he became a resident in Crookston Care Home, Cardonald, Glasgow.

We are indebted to Allison O'Neill, who worked as a newly qualified nurse at the care home and was Arthur's key worker. The 22-year-old was taken with the ageing veteran, whom she found gentle and courteous. She was impressed by Arthur's cheerfulness, smart appearance and the fact he was clearly very well read. Arthur brought with him – to be given pride of place in the residents' lounge – two large-scale models he'd built from scratch, one of the *Royal Scot* (presumably the LMS Royal Scot Class 7P 4-6-0) and the other of the *Queen Mary* (launched September 1934). Arthur mentioned he had worked on the construction of that iconic vessel.

The new resident had lost none of his sparkle, remaining constantly sociable and gregarious, with his craft skills much in demand. No football fan, he preferred cricket, which Allison attributed to his English origins! She recalls that he did not have the distinctive Glasgow accent, despite having lived in and being very much part of the city for most of his life. As he grew older it seems the Great War was much on his mind. He shunned war films but would talk, if asked, about his war experiences and became very emotional on Remembrance Day.

He was neither mawkish nor sentimental, though he did often talk about his wife, whom he loved very much. Strangely, he never mentioned any other relatives. His health was steadily deteriorating. A lifelong pipe smoker, he suffered from emphysema and his recurring foot problems – that long legacy of the trenches – limited his mobility. Latterly he walked with the aid of a Zimmer frame.

Allison formed the impression that Arthur might have been a freemason, though we have no evidence for this. He was certainly helpful and considerate towards his fellow residents, particularly one afflicted by blindness, Maxwell Pauline, whom he befriended and mentored and who was later inconsolable after Arthur died. As long as he was able, he remained a regular churchgoer.

In January 1982, as storm clouds gathered over the South Atlantic and a new war threatened, this quiet veteran of the 'war to end all wars' contracted a severe cold and began, at the age of 84, to prepare for his final battle. Allison was with Arthur when, on 15 January 1982, he died, as he had lived, with unostentatious dignity.

The only time Allison witnessed Arthur's anger was when he had to rescue her from violent assault by a mentally ill resident. The old soldier was outraged, even though Allison explained the assailant was not really responsible for his actions. As Arthur came to the rescue the attacker hurled an accusation – 'What have you ever done in your life?' She tells us the comment brought on a 'contemplative' mood. We speculate it may have been this experience towards the end of his long life that prompted Arthur finally to gather up his treasured memorabilia, which had travelled with him throughout his life, and place them all in the security of 'The Box'.

Throughout our voyage of discovery we have come to think, through handling the collection of Arthur's lifelong worldly goods and in unearthing and understanding some of their significances, that in some way, we knew Arthur Roberts, although, clearly we never did.

Arthur was a man Robert Burns would have known as 'A Common Man' – to those who knew him, 'A Good Man', and to all those who have read his story, 'A Humble Man', who's friendship, if we had been allowed it, would have been valued, respected and lauded.

Arthur Roberts, like so many of those who went through the Great War, was at once both an ordinary man and yet very extraordinary. He and his generation passed through a fire we cannot even begin to imagine. Whatever revisionist historians may decide upon the necessity for the war or the validity of the sacrifice, it was real and they believed it to be both right and just. We must salute them. The expression 'hero' is much overworked at present and no veteran this author has ever encountered has described himself or has desired to be described as such. The late distinguished American writer Stephen E. Ambrose, in his *Pegasus Bridge* (1994), on interviewing one of the British VCs (holders of the Victoria Cross), is cautioned by his subject not to make the man out as any kind of hero. The writer memorably responded that he didn't make heroes, he merely wrote about them. We are now privileged to be able to do the same. As good as any man – no room for doubt. It seems fitting to let somebody who knew Arthur well have the final word:

Although it has been over thirty years since Arthur passed away I have never forgotten him. Not only was he an artist, a musician, a model maker and a skilled workman, he was a dignified and very thoughtful man, who always had a smile on his face. He was a great inspiration to me and I loved him dearly.

I believe the thoughts in his diary, his memoirs and his reminiscences are his voice from the grave and will immortalise him forever. He would be so proud today to know that his musings are to be made public. We now can share the memories of this honourable soldier, husband and friend. I for one will be the first in the queue to read his book.

Thank you for bringing back some very happy memories of a wonderful, caring, quiet and lovable man.

Allison O'Neill.

THIRD BATTLE OF YPRES 1917

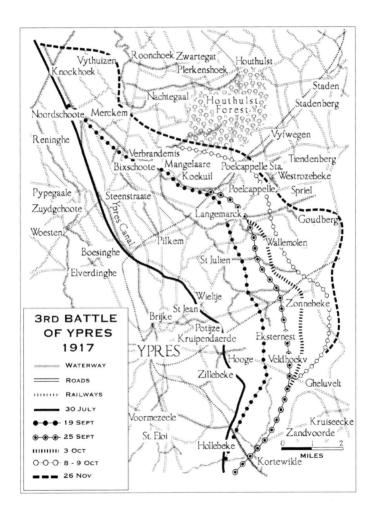

WESTERN FRONT 1914–18

BIBLIOGRAPHY

Primary Sources

Roberts, Arthur, *Diary*
Roberts, Arthur, *Memoirs*
Roberts, Arthur, *Reminiscences*
War Diary 2nd Battalion RSF (1917)

Secondary sources

Bailey, Brigadier J.B.A., 'Deep Battle 1914–1941: The Birth of the Modern Style of Warfare', *British Army Review*, no. 120
Bailey, Brigadier J.B.A., 'The Century of Firepower', *British Army Review*, no. 120
Baynes, J., *Morale* (London, 1967)
Beech, Dr J., MBE, 'The Division in the Attack', 1918, SS135, T/1635, 40/WO/7036 (Strategic and Combat Studies Institute, *The Occasional*, no. 53)
Blunden, E., *Undertones of War* (London, 1965)
Brittain, V., *Testament of Youth* (London, 1978)
Buchan, J., *The History of the Royal Scots Fusiliers 1678–1918* (London, 1920)
Chandler, D.G. (ed.), *The Oxford Illustrated History of the British Army* (Oxford, 1994)
Clarke, A., *The Donkeys* (London, 1991)
Clayton, A., *The British Officer* (Harlow, 2007)
Corrigan, Major G., *Mud, Blood & Poppycock* (London, 2003)
Dunn, J.C., *The War the Infantry Knew* (London, 1988)
Elder, G.W., *From Geordie Land to No-Man's-Land* (Indiana, 2011)
Ellis, J., *Eye Deep in Hell* (London, 1976)
Falls, C., *The First World War* (London, 1960)

Ferguson, N., *The Pity of War* (London, 2006)

Giddings, R., *The War Poets* (London, 1988)

Gilbert, A., *Sniper: One on One* (London, 1994)

Gladden, N., *Ypres 1917* (London, 1967)

Graves, R., *Goodbye to All That* (London, 1969)

Holmes, R., *The Western Front* (London, 1999)

Keegan, Sir J., *The Face of Battle* (London, 2004)

Keegan, Sir J., *The First World War* (London, 1978)

Laffin, J. (ed.), *Letters from the Front* (London, 1973)

MacArthur, B. (ed.), *For King & Country* (London, 2008)

Macmillan, H., *The Winds of Change* (London, 1966)

Marrion, R.J., and D.S.V. Potten, *The British Army 1914–1918*, Osprey 'Men-At-Arms' no. 81 (Oxford, 1978)

Martin, B., *Poor Bloody Infantry: A Subaltern on the Western Front* (London, 1987)

Pound, R., *The Lost Generation* (London, 1964)

Sheffield, G., *Leadership in the Trenches* (London, 2000)

Thompson, Major-General J., *Setting the Record Straight – the Douglas Haig Fellowship Lecture*, 21 June 2010

Walker, G. (ed.), *In Flanders Fields* (London, 2004)

INDEX

If you enjoyed this book, you may also be interested in …

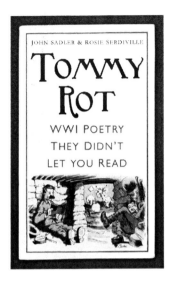

Tommy Rot

The First World War produced a large corpus of war poetry, though focus to date has rested with the 'big' names – Brooke, Sassoon, Graves, Owen, Rosenberg and Blunden et al. However, there are others that, until now, you would not expect to find in any Great War anthology. This is 'Tommy' verse, mainly written by other ranks and not, as is generally the case with the more famous war poets, by officers. It is, much of it, doggerel, loaded with lavatorial humour, with a raw immediacy, and an instant connection that the reader will find compelling.

9780752492087

Ode to Bully Beef

The Second World War was not greeted with the same lavish outpouring of patriotic fervour that had attended August 1914. Any rags of glory had long since been drowned in the mud of Flanders. Death sought new victims everywhere; British citizens were now in the front line, there was no respite, no hiding place. This is the poetry and prose of those who were there, ordinary people caught in the terrible maelstrom of mass conflict on a scale hitherto unimagined; this is their testimony.

9780752491899

Visit our website and discover thousands of other History Press books.

www.thehistorypress.co.uk